Ask Gramps

Addressing 101 Everyday
Concerns, Curiosities, and
Uncertainties of Latter-day Saints,
Young and Old

~VOLUME 1~

H. Clay Gorton

Maasai, Inc.
Provo, Utah

*"To my inquisitive granddaughter,
Thalia Gorton Anderson,
who started it all."*

Published by Maasai, Inc.
201 East Bay Blvd
Provo, Utah 84606

Front cover graphic design by Douglass Cole, Orem, Utah.
Page design by www.SunriseBooks.com

2001 edition by Maasai, Inc.
Library of Congress Control Number: 2001116253
ISBN: 0-9708008-6-X

Other Titles by H. Clay Gorton

LANGUAGE OF THE LORD
Horizon Publishers, August 1993, 351 pages
New discoveries of Chiasma in the Doctrine & Covenants

THE LEGACY OF THE BRASS PLATES OF LABAN
Horizon Publishers, November 1994, 298 pages
A comparison of Biblical and Book of Mormon Isaiah texts

A NEW WITNESS FOR CHRIST
Horizon Publishers, March 1997, 478 pages
Chiastic structures in the Book of Mormon

SUBJECT INDEX

Foreword

"Ask Gramps" started as an effort by Clay Gorton to communicate with his grandchildren via the Internet and answer their doctrinal questions. His column was soon picked up by Mormon Town (www.mormontown.org) and quickly became a favorite. Now, Gorton may have one of the largest audiences and forums in The Church of Jesus Christ of Latter-day Saints—and it's worldwide! "Gramps," as he is affectionately called, is more than qualified. He has had extensive experience in counseling others in the capacity of bishop, stake president, mission president and MTC president. His years of answering questions about doctrine have provided him a library of information that he has carefully catalogued. Drawing people to the scriptures and the words of the prophets has been his trademark, carefully guiding the questioner to deep meanings and sublime truths.

Accolades are constant:

"You are a gold mine!"

"That is positively the best explanation I've been given to date. I hope you don't mind if I print this out and share it."

"On your answer concerning headlights and light speed, may I say I've never read a more eloquent explanation. What I found most interesting was your comment on where the theory of relativity will end up. It is, after all, just a theory! Given that technology is approximately doubling every six months, we arrive at an exponential equation that boggles the mind of anyone born near the turn of the last century."

"I enjoy Mormon Town—the *Ask Gramps* feature is probably my favorite. I have told many of my friends about your site. Thank you so much."

"I love your explanations of things. They are simple and straightforward, yet never stuffy."

"How did you get so smart? I would be happy if you adopted me as your grandson."

"Gramps, I think you do a wonderful job. Your answers are thorough, understandable, referenced by standard works and general authorities, and therefore doctrinally sound. I appreciate the fact that many of them are loving and kind to the writer."

"Gramps, when do you plan on publishing a book of all the questions you have received, and your replies?"

Well, here it is—a wonderful collection of questions answered by a true gospel scholar. Witty, fun, informative, inspiring—a great gift for anyone, young or old.
Enjoy!

—*Larry Barkdull,*
author and publisher

WHY DIDN'T GOD PREVENT ADAM AND EVE FROM PARTAKING OF THE FORBIDDEN FRUIT?

Gramps,

This has been a question that I have thought about over and over through the years. In Genesis, Abraham, and Moses we read about Adam and Eve partaking of the Tree of Knowledge of Good and Evil. As we know, they were told not to—however, they could use their agency to decide. We also know the decision that was made, and how it happened, and the consequences that came from that act. Before Heavenly Father sent them out of the garden, He placed Cherubim and a flaming sword east in the Garden of Eden to protect them from eating of the Tree of Life so that they would not live forever in their sins. This is the question: why didn't He just make that decision in the beginning and place cherubim and a flaming sword around the Tree of Knowledge of good and evil ? They had their agency—this I know—but was their agency not taken from them in regards to eating of the Tree of Life by the cherubim protecting it from them? It seems God said they could use their agency in one respect and could not in another respect.

Sandy

Dear Sandy,

Your question seems to be concerning the extent to which the Lord granted free agency to Adam and Eve. There are perhaps a couple of things that might be considered. Before the fall, Adam and Eve were immortal. Had they not partaken of the forbidden fruit they would have lived forever. Partaking of the Tree of Life in that condition would probably have done nothing to change their state as they were already immortal. So there would have been no reason to protect them from it at that time.

You ask, why did He not keep them from partaking of the Tree of Knowledge of Good and Evil? For man to exercise his agency he must be faced with meaningful choices. When Eve succumbed to temptation and partook of the fruit, by which act she became mortal (subject to death) and would be expelled from the garden, Adam was faced with a meaningful choice. He could obey one commandment or the other, but not both. He could remain alone in his immortal state in the Garden of Eden or he could choose to become mortal and go with Eve in order to fulfill the commandment to multiply and replenish the earth. We learn in 1 Timothy 2:14 that

Adam was not deceived, but the woman being deceived was in the transgression.

The purpose of Adam and Eve coming to this earth was to begin its population so that the spirit children of our Father in Heaven could advance from their first estate (in the pre-mortal spirit world) to their second estate, mortality. (See Abr. 3:25-26) Had the Lord not permitted Eve to partake of the fruit of the Tree of knowledge Good and Evil, in opposition to His commandment, they would not have become mortal, and the human family on this earth could not have been.

It is interesting to note that on each of the worlds peopled by our Father's children, there have been an Adam and an Eve.

> *And the first man of all men have I called Adam, which is many.* (Moses 1:34)

> *And Adam called his wife's name Eve, because she was the mother of all living; for thus have I, the Lord God, called the first of all women, which are many.* (Moses 4:26)

—Gramps

WHY ISN'T THE BOOK OF MORMON ORDERED CHRONOLOGICALLY?

Dear Gramps,
Why does the Book of Mormon skip around in its dates going from A.D. to B.C. and vice versa, instead of just going in order?
Melanie & Shelly

Dear Melanie & Shelly,

The Book of Mormon is an account of the family of Lehi who left Jerusalem for the Promised Land in 600 B.C. and his descendants. After some time his descendants divided into two groups, the Nephites and the Lamanites. About 470 years after their arrival, the Nephites living in Zarahemla discovered a man by the name of Coriantumr, "and he did dwell with them for the space of nine moons." (Omni 1:21) Coriantumr was a descendant of the Jaredites, who migrated to the Promised Land from the Tower of Babel after the confounding of tongues about 2247 B.C.

The record of the Jaredite people was discovered by Ammon and his group while on an excursion to learn about the people living in the land of

Nephi-Lehi, from which they had previously emigrated. Several years before Ammon's excursion, a man by the name of Zeniff took a number of people with him and returned to Nephi-Lehi to live. Ammon found his descendants there, living as captors of the Lamanites.

The prophet Mormon, born about 311 A.D., abridged the records that had been kept by the kings and prophets of the Nephites since the time of Nephi. He also added his own record to the account. However, he was killed in battle before the work was complete, and his son, Moroni, finished his father's record, then made an abridgement of the record of the Jaredites, and finally added his own account, called the Book of Moroni.

This is just the briefest of thumbnail sketches of the thousand-year history of these two great nations. Now, think of a historian of our day writing the history of England and its people including their migrations and conquests beginning at 1000 A.D. Do you think such a historian could write that complicated account without going back and forth in time as he chronicled one group and then another that had come out of Briton? In the same way the Book of Mormon account cannot be strictly chronological because it follows the accounts of different groups of contemporary people.

—Gramps

DO OBITUARIES CONTAIN FALSE DOCTRINE?

Dear Gramps,

While reading the daily newspaper, I often stop at the obituaries to look at the pictures and read some of the things written about the deceased individuals. Sometimes seeing the picture of small children or young adults makes me pause and feel sympathy for those who have lost a loved one at such a young age. However, I am more disturbed by the inference in the obituary that many such individuals have "gone home to live with their Heavenly Father," (a distinction rarely given to those who have lived long lives. Most obituaries about the elderly simply say "passed away.") We know that the spirit world is here on earth, and despite the comfort such language may give for the survivors, should we really be suggesting that after we die, we fall into the Savior's arms or "go home" to our Father in Heaven? I know there are stories of near-death experiences and renderings depicting this sort of reunion with deity, but is there really some magic in death that makes us worthy to look upon the face of Christ or God even if

we hadn't or weren't able to do so before death? I would like to hear what you have to say on the subject. Thank you.
  Darrel in Provo

Dear Darrel,
  It appears that we are not left alone when we pass into the next compartment. Alma says,

> Now, concerning the state of the soul between death and the resurrection—Behold, it has been made known unto me by an angel, that the spirits of all men, as soon as they are departed from this mortal body, yea, the spirits of all men, whether they be good or evil, are taken home to that God who gave them life. (Alma 40:11)

That does not mean that we remain in God's presence. Alma continues—

> And then shall it come to pass, that the spirits of those who are righteous are received into a state of happiness, which is called paradise, a state of rest, a state of peace, where they shall rest from all their troubles and from all care, and sorrow.
> And then shall it come to pass, that the spirits of the wicked, yea, who are evil—for behold, they have no part nor portion of the Spirit of the Lord; for behold, they chose evil works rather than good; therefore the spirit of the devil did enter into them, and take possession of their house— and these shall be cast out into outer darkness; there shall be weeping, and wailing, and gnashing of teeth, and this because of their own iniquity, being led captive by the will of the devil. (Alma 40:12-13)

So there is an element of truth in the obituaries that you refer to. However, apart from that, the deep emotions that are felt when a loved one passes away, are given expression in words of hope and consolation. Perhaps we should look more toward the feelings of the bereaved ones than to the technical accuracy of their epitaphs.
  —Gramps

WHY DO CATS ALWAYS LAND ON THEIR FEET?

Hi Gramps,
  I was just wondering how cats always land on their feet? If you could answer me this, I would greatly appreciate it!
  Mormon Child

Dear Mormon Child,

Short answer:

Cats always land on their feet because they don't want to break their necks.

Extended Answer:

If toast always lands buttered-side down, and cats always land on their feet, what happens if you strap toast on the back of a cat and drop it? After a great deal of experimentation, in which I used up two loaves of bread, a tub of butter, and quite a few cats, I can say that the results are inconclusive. Eighty percent of the time, the cat landed on its feet. I suspected however that this might be due to the disproportion in the cat/buttered-toast masses. Increasing the number of slices of buttered toast as well as decreasing the size of the cat seemed to bear this supposition out. The closer the relative weights of cat/buttered toast approached 1:1, the more the initial drop configuration (i.e. cat up or down) seemed to influence the landing. My conclusion was that buttered toast didn't work.

My observations, however, inspired me to try strapping two cats back-to-back and dropping them. I discovered that if you work from a sufficient height (a second-story balcony seems to do nicely), 30% of the time one of the cats lands on its feet; however, in the other 70% of the trials, the two cats land on their sides. This confirmed my observations of the cat/buttered toast experiments, that the assemblage was capable of rotating under its own power as it fell. In other words, angular momentum was being generated, and this suggested that, if it could be harnessed, it might prove to be a source of relatively clean and cheap energy.

I tested this hypothesis a few times with four cats strapped to a 4-by-4 beam dropped from a height of ten meters. Unfortunately the muscular energy of just four cats proved to be insufficient to cause the mass of the beam to rotate at all. An 8-cp (eight cat-power), assemblage with a four-cat array strapped at either end of such a beam should, in theory, work; but trials have revealed that, with this many cats involved, their individual efforts to land feet-first are canceled out because the cats don't all try to right themselves in the same direction or at the same time. Although some angular motion does occur, it is erratic at best.

I intend to continue this research by experimenting with lighter, composite-material beams and also with better ways of timing and coordinating cat-effort delivery and will be getting on with it just as soon as the suspicions of the neighborhood's (former) cat-owners have been allayed and a new supply of cats is available.

—Gramps

IS GENEALOGY AN OBSESSION?

Dear Gramps,
I'm a member of the church and I have a question. My wife and I got in to a heated discussion about my wish to do genealogy and she says that I'm obsessing over it. The question is, what is crossing the line of obsession and hobby? I really don't know! My wife says I do genealogy once a week. And that is about right. Is that an obsession with genealogy?
Jared

Dear Jared,

Perhaps your problem is not how much time you spend doing genealogy, but how much time you spend doing things with your wife. I imagine her concern is not that you are doing genealogy *per se,* but that you are not doing something else. What would she have you do instead of doing genealogy? If you could satisfy that need, it may be that there would be no concern over how much time you spend doing other things.

The work we do in seeking after our ancestors is to provide for them the blessings of the gospel that they cannot now provide for themselves. An appropriate place to start in genealogy is to provide for the spiritual welfare of the ancestors of our descendants—in other words, ourselves. If you could assure the happiness and welfare of your wife so that there would be no place in your relationship for heated arguments, I would imagine that there would then be the time and interest to do genealogy together.

—Gramps

IS IT HARDER TO ACCEPT THE GOSPEL IN THE SPIRIT WORLD?

Dear Gramps,
Some say it is somewhat more difficult to accept the gospel in the spirit world while another school of thought says it would be much easier inasmuch as we would have more knowledge after we pass through the veil. I was wondering which is correct.
Paul from Kentucky

Dear Paul,

When we pass through the veil we are the same person that we were in mortality. The mind is of the spirit and the brain is the physical entity that houses the mind. At death the mind, as part of the spirit, enters the spirit world. We are the same persons we were before, with the same likes and dislikes, with the same passions and desires. The vices of the flesh may not be satisfied in the spirit world. The drunkard will have the same longing for drink, but no way to satisfy that longing. Will repentance be easier or more difficult? Who is to say? How can we judge another even when we are familiar with the person's surroundings? How much more difficult it would be to try to judge how a person would react to the teachings of the gospel in an environment that we know nothing about. Some thoughts on the subject, written by the General Authorities, might be worth considering—

So-called deathbed repentance is not part of the divine plan. It is an attempt to live after the manner of the world during the years of vigor and virility, and then to gain the rewards of the blessed without ever overcoming the lusts of the flesh, lusts that, with old age and death, cease to burn in the mortal soul. Thus Amulek continues:

Do not procrastinate the day of your repentance until the end; for after this day of life, which is given us to prepare for eternity, behold, if we do not improve our time while in this life then cometh the night of darkness wherein there can be no labor performed.

There are no redeeming doctrines, no saving ordinances, no promised kingdoms of glory for such. Those who reject the gospel in this life—having heard the word from the lips of a legal administrator and having been made aware of its glories and truths—and who then accept it in the spirit world shall go to the terrestrial kingdom. (Bruce R. McConkie, *A New Witness for the Articles of Faith,* p. 230)

There is another question that arises here. If men can hear the Gospel in the spirit world, can they obey it fully in the spirit world? Let us look at that a little. Here are the Gospel ordinances. Are ordinances of any effect? Yes, they are. 'Except a man be born of water and of the Spirit, he cannot enter into the Kingdom of God.' Just the same as if an alien does not obey the naturalization laws he cannot become a citizen of the United States. God's house is a house of order. He has a way of His own, and he that will not accept that way cannot obtain the blessing. Then can those spirits who hear the Gospel in the spirit world obey the Gospel fully? Can they believe? Yes. Can they repent? Why not? It is the soul of man, or the spirit of man in the body, not the body, that believes. It is the spirit of man in the body that repents. What is it that obeys the ordinances? Why, the spirit. But these ordinances belong to this sphere in which we live, they belong to the earth, they belong to the flesh. Water is an earthly element composed of two gases. It belongs to this earth. What there is in the spirit world, we know little about. But here is the water in which repentant believers must be baptized. Can they be baptized in the spirit world? It appears not. (Charles W. Penrose, *Journal of Discourses,* Vol.24, p.96-97)

—Gramps

ARE TRIBAL DECLARATIONS NECESSARY
IN A PATRIARCHAL BLESSING?

Dear Gramps,

I have two questions about lineage as revealed to an individual in a patriarchal blessing.

First question: Is it necessary to have a tribe designated? Neither my husband nor I have a tribe of Israel designated in our patriarchal blessings. These blessings were given thousands of miles and many years apart long before we even knew each other. We are both told we are of the house of Israel but that is all. Is this adequate? If not, what do we need to do?

Second question: What is the difference between the blessings, assignments, etc. of the tribes of Ephraim and Manasseh? I have heard that during the Millennium, Ephraim will have the responsibility of missionary work while Manasseh will be charged with temple work. Do you know if this is correct? If so, do you know where I can find a reference regarding it? We have nine children; four are of Ephraim and five are of Manasseh. Because of this we are interested in knowing more about what the different tribal designations mean. Thanks for your help.

Cheryl, Provo, UT

Dear Cheryl,

It is common that the specific lineages within the house of Israel be given in patriarchal blessings. It would not be inappropriate to approach your stake patriarch and refer the question to him.

With regard to different assignments for the tribes of Ephraim and Manasseh during the Millennium, I know of no scripture that makes a distinction. All members of the Church are missionaries. Brigham Young said that "there is neither man or woman in this church who is not on a mission." (DBY 322) We further understand that all of our Father's children will have the opportunity to hear and accept, if they will, the principles of the gospel of Jesus Christ, either in mortality or beyond the veil. We read in D&C 90:11 that

> *it shall come to pass in that day, that every man shall hear the fulness of the gospel in his own tongue, and in his own language, through those who are ordained unto this power, by the administration of the Comforter, shed forth upon them for the revelation of Jesus Christ.*

However, not every one in every nation will hear the gospel preached. But to all those who will not have had the opportunity to know the gospel in this life, it will be taught to them in the post-mortal spirit world. (See D&C 138:31-32) Undoubtedly such a great task is not now nor will be restricted to the tribe of Ephraim.

Now the great work of the Millennium will be to provide for all the saving ordinances to be performed in holy temples for all those who accept the gospel in the spirit world following their mortal sojourn. Brigham Young declares that this great work is to be done by the seed of Abraham, not by only one of the tribes of Israel.

> As I have frequently told you, that is the work of the Millennium. It is the work that has to be performed by the seed of Abraham, the chosen seed, the royal seed, the blessed of the Lord, those the Lord made covenants with. They will step forth, and save every son and daughter of Adam who will receive salvation here on the earth; and all the spirits in the spirit world will be preached to, conversed with, and the principles of salvation carried to them, that they may have the privilege of receiving the Gospel; and they will have plenty of children here on the earth to officiate for them in those ordinances of the Gospel that pertain to the flesh. (*DBY* 403)

If we live faithfully, keeping the commandments, the Lord will direct our labors in the Kingdom through those who hold the keys of priesthood authority. If we respond to the requests for service from our bishops, quorum presidents and stake presidents, we may know that we will be on the Lord's errand, doing what He would have us do to build up the kingdom of God on the earth and helping to establish the cause of Zion.

—Gramps

WHY WOULD A MISSIONARY
BE RELEASED EARLY?

Dear Gramps,

We had a friend who left the MTC after only 1 week. He was given an honorable release. Why would the authorities at the MTC not try any harder than that to keep him on his mission? What is he to expect his standing to be in the LDS community?

Janet

Dear Janet,

There are numbers of reasons why a missionary might be dismissed from the MTC. They could involve questions of health and attitude as well as worthiness. It is appropriate that the details of such matters be kept confidential.

I cannot imagine that the authorities at the MTC would not have done all that was appropriate for the welfare of the missionary. The well being of the missionary is the paramount responsibility of the MTC authorities and the mission presidents. I believe that you can rest assured that the missionary in question was treated with loving kindness, and was given every opportunity to continue according to the protocol and standards related to missionary service.

In making judgments where the details of the circumstance are not known, it would be far better to err on the side of the assumption that all concerned acted in accordance with their responsibilities and the principals of the gospel, rather than on the side that there was some fault or deficiency on the part of those responsible for the decisions that were made.

The boy's standing in the LDS community, I imagine, will depend more on the integrity of the LDS community than on any implications of some possible wrongdoing on the part of the boy. If he is judged and rejected because of some imagined fault, those who act in such a harsh manner are far worse off than the person that they are judging. The Lord has spoken directly to this matter, as follows:

> *Wherefore, I say unto you, that ye ought to forgive one another; for he that forgiveth not his brother his trespasses standeth condemned before the Lord; for there remaineth in him the greater sin.* (D&C 64:9)

—Gramps

WHO WILL SAVE AMERICA?

Gramps,
Who will save America? President Hinckley stated that the Latter-day
Saints will be the ones to save America. Is this statement true?
CJ Newton

Dear CJ,
President Hinckley was probably referring to the statement made by
Joseph Smith and recorded by Brigham Young, as follows:

> Will the Constitution be destroyed? No; it will be held inviolate by
> this people; and, as Joseph Smith said, "The time will come when the des-
> tiny of the nation will hang upon a single thread. At this critical juncture,
> this people will step forth and save it from the threatened destruction."
> (*Discourses of Brigham Young*, p.469)

By the word "people" the prophet was referring to the members of the
Church. This is obvious from the words of President Ezra Taft Benson, who
said,

> The Lord told the Prophet Joseph Smith there would be an attempt to
> overthrow the country by destroying the Constitution. Joseph Smith pre-
> dicted that the time would come when the Constitution would hang, as it
> were, by a thread, and at that time "this people will step forth and save it
> from the threatened destruction." (*Journal of Discourses*, 7:15) It is my
> conviction that the elders of Israel, widely spread over the nation, will at
> that crucial time successfully rally the righteous of our country and pro-
> vide the necessary balance of strength to save the institutions of constitu-
> tional government. (*Teachings of Ezra Taft Benson*, p.618-619)

—Gramps

WHY DOES GOD SEND RETARDED
CHILDREN INTO THE WORLD?

Dear Gramps,
We have a daughter who has Down Syndrome. At times she is a joy, but
at all times she is a heavy responsibility. Why does God send such children
into the world, especially profoundly retarded ones who will never be able
to care for themselves?
Ron

Dear Ron,

And as Jesus passed by, he saw a man which was blind from his birth. And his disciples asked him, saying, Master, who did sin, this man, or his parents, that he was born blind? Jesus answered, Neither hath this man sinned, nor his parents: but that the works of God should be made manifest in him. (John 9:1-3)

Here is the prime example of why the Lord would bring into the world handicapped children. But how are the works of God manifest through those who care for their disadvantaged children? One of the noblest endeavors of man is to care for the less fortunate. The Savior again gave the example when He told of the good Shepherd who left without care the ninety and nine and went searching for the one that was lost.

I suppose that we were not unaware in the pre-mortal spirit world of what life would be like in mortality. I could imagine that you had made a pact with your child who in that state would have volunteered to come into mortality in a disadvantaged condition to give you the opportunity to care for her and thus reap the rich blessings promised to those who sacrifice themselves in compassionate service to others.

Henry Drummond, in his little treatise on love entitled "The Greatest Thing In The World," made this cogent statement:

"The greatest thing," says someone, "a man can do for his Heavenly Father is to be kind to some of His other children." I wonder why it is that we are not all kinder than we are. How much the world needs it. How easily it is done. How instantaneously it acts. How infallibly it is remembered. How superabundantly it pays itself back—for there is no debtor in the world so honorable, so superbly honorable, as Love.

It is interesting to consider in light of your situation the principles of priesthood power and influence as found in D&C 121:41-42:

No power or influence can or ought to be maintained by virtue of the priesthood, only by persuasion, by long-suffering, by gentleness and meekness, and by love unfeigned; By kindness, and pure knowledge.

Think of these principles of priesthood power and influence—persuasion, long-suffering, gentleness, meekness, love unfeigned and kindness. They don't just happen to us; they must be acquired and developed by life's experiences and by how we respond to them. Someone said, "Authority can never be acquired, it must always be conferred; while ability can never by conferred, it must always be acquired."

However, so often when we are faced with unpleasant or difficult circumstances, we ask the question, "Why Me?" The immediate answer is

"Why not you?" Rather than asking "Why me?" we should fall on our knees and thank the Lord for the sacred opportunity that He has given us to become more like He is. Here are some of His promises to those who have the strength to be called upon to undergo difficult and trying circumstances during their mortal sojourn:

> *Search diligently, pray always, and be believing, and all things shall work together for your good, if ye walk uprightly and remember the covenant wherewith ye have covenanted one with another.* (D&C 90:24)

> *Verily I say unto you, all among them who know their hearts are honest, and are broken, and their spirits contrite, and are willing to observe their covenants by sacrifice—yea, every sacrifice which I, the Lord, shall command—they are accepted of me. For I, the Lord, will cause them to bring forth as a very fruitful tree which is planted in a goodly land, by a pure stream, that yieldeth much precious fruit.* (D&C 97:8-9)

> *Therefore, he giveth this promise unto you, with an immutable covenant that they shall be fulfilled; and all things wherewith you have been afflicted shall work together for your good, and to my name's glory, saith the Lord.* (D&C 98:3)

> *For after much tribulation, as I have said unto you in a former commandment, cometh the blessing.* (D&C 103:12)

—Gramps

WHY DO WE ALL SAY AMEN?

Gramps,

Do we always have to say "amen" after the person praying has said "amen"? And after a talk is given and they say "in the name of Jesus, amen," do we have to say "amen" again or is it something that we just do? And if so why?

Eva

Dear Eva,

The repeating of "amen" by the congregation after a prayer or a discourse is a very old custom, dating from biblical times. The Hebrew word "amen" was adopted into the Greek language, then into the Latin language, and came into the English language before the 12th century. The word "amen" in the Hebrew means "so be it." It has the same meaning in Greek when used at the end of a prayer or discourse. However, in Greek it may be used at the beginning of a discourse, to mean "surely, truly, of a truth."

The repeating of the word by members of the congregation is their affirmation of what was said—a verbal expression of concurrence or agreement. So it is customary and appropriate in our Church meetings to voice approval of the prayer or discourse by repeating the word "amen."

The practice varies from congregation to congregation. In some wards one hears an enthusiastic response by the congregation. In others, no verbal expression is heard. This indicates that the practice is somewhat habitual, and the members tend to follow along with the established practice. It would seem appropriate for us to listen carefully to the prayers that are offered and to the talks that are given, so that at the end we could voice our support, approval and concurrence with what was spoken and our commitment to comply with the counsel given.

—Gramps

DOES SATAN CONTROL OF THE WATERS?

Dear Gramps,

Since my early years, my mother would often tell me that Satan controls all waters, which is why missionaries aren't allowed to swim while serving. I served a mission in Arkansas a few years back and remember quite vividly several not-so-righteous elders and sisters at a member's home swimming. Is there a scriptural reference to Satan's having control? Thanks!

Tom

Dear Tom,

As you know, missionaries serve under regulations that would be considered rather severe by those who are not acquainted with the work. However, as they are called on the Lord's errand, and their service is so vital to the eternal salvation of our Father's children, they are encouraged to dedicate all their time and talents to the work of the Lord. A weekly preparation day is provided, however, so that essential duties not primarily related to the missionary work itself may be accomplished. This is not primarily a recreation day, although conservative recreational activities are permitted and even encouraged.

However, not only is swimming prohibited, but also other activities that may be either dangerous or not within the spirit of their calling. Missionaries should be particularly circumspect about activities "on the waters," as there is indeed both scriptural and historic precedent for avoiding unnecessary exposure.

On 9 August, 1831, the Prophet Joseph Smith, with ten elders of the Church, began a journey from Independence, Missouri to Kirtland, Ohio. The prophet recorded the following about this experience in his journal:

> Many of the dangers so common upon the western waters, manifested themselves; and after we had encamped upon the bank of the river, at McIlwaine's Bend, Brother Phelps, in open vision by daylight, saw the destroyer in his most terrible power, ride upon the face of the waters; others heard the noise, but saw not the vision. (Joseph Fielding Smith, *Church History and Modern Revelation*, Vol 1, p. 206)

Following the recording of this account, on August 12, the prophet received the revelation identified as Section 61 in the Doctrine and Covenants. Part of that revelation refers specifically to the power of the adversary "upon the waters."

> *Behold, I, the Lord, in the beginning blessed the waters; but in the last days, by the mouth of my servant John, I cursed the waters. Wherefore, the days will come that no flesh shall be safe upon the waters. And it shall be said in days to come that none is able to go up to the land of Zion upon the waters, but he that is upright in heart....And now I give unto you a commandment that what I say unto one I say unto all, that you shall forewarn your brethren concerning these waters, that they come not in journeying upon them, lest their faith fail and they are caught in snares; I, the Lord, have decreed, and the destroyer rideth upon the face thereof, and I revoke not the decree. Wherefore, let those concerning whom I have spoken, that should take their journey in haste—again I say unto you, let them take their journey in haste. And it mattereth not unto me, after a little, if it so be that they fill their mission, whether they go by water or by land; let this be as it is made known unto them according to their judgments hereafter.* (D&C 61:14-22)

We read that *it mattereth not unto me, after a little, if it so be that they fill their mission, whether they go by water or by land*. One could infer from the above that those who were on their mission at this time should not travel by water, but that after their mission they could travel either by water or by land. Also, we read that the days will come when only those who are *upright in heart* would be able to journey on the waters. These are not the only dangers that could befall those who are not upright in heart. Those who persist in disobeying the Lord's commands would eventually lose the influence of the Holy Spirit and would come under the power and control of the Adversary. Alma tells us,

> *And they that will harden their hearts, to them is given the lesser por-*
> *tion of the word until they know nothing concerning his mysteries; and*
> *then they are taken captive by the devil, and led by his will down to*
> *destruction. Now this is what is meant by the chains of hell.* (Alma 12:11)

—Gramps

IF THE WORLD IS ONLY 6,000 YEARS OLD, HOW DO WE EXPLAIN DINOSAUR BONES?

Gramps,
I have had numerous people ask me about the dinosaur bones and the
age of the earth. I am not sure what book I read, I think Gospel Doctrine,
but it stated the earth as being only 5,000 to 6,000 years old. If so, how can
bones be found that date back millions of years? I have been told that the
earth was created from existing matter that had the bones in it. Any ideas
on how to answer this question? Thanks,
nknight

Dear nknight,
The reference to 6,000 years is not the age at which the earth was created, but the time since it was transformed from a terrestrial to a telestial
kingdom, which took place at the fall of Adam.

No chronological data is given in the scriptures concerning the age of
the earth. We have no information on how long Adam and Eve and the
plants and animals lived on the earth prior to its transformation into a telestial kingdom. However, we do know that death was not introduced in the
earth until after the expulsion of Adam and Eve from the Garden of Eden,
which would have occurred about 4000 B.C.

There are two factors that throw into question geological and anthro-
pological dating estimates. One: Those estimates are all based on the theory that the earth has had a benign history, i.e., the earth's present state has
been achieved as the result of very gradual aging processes—erosion from
wind, water, freezing and thawing, and from the gradual continental uplift
from internal pressures.

It is apparent, even to the casual observer, that the earth has not had a
benign history, but rather, a very catastrophic one where major changes in
topography have occurred as a result of cataclysmic events.

Carbon dating, for instance, which is accurate to only a few thousand
years, presupposes a consistent fraction of carbon dioxide in the atmosphere

and a constant ratio of the radioactive carbon 14 to the stable carbon 12. These factors could be affected by major volcanic upheavals and by the near passage of relatively large astronomical bodies in which there could have been exchange of material between the earth and the passing body. Other methods of measuring geological time also depend the assumption of constant factors in the measuring process.

But apart from all that, factor number two: Brigham Young reveals that before the fall of Adam the earth was not a member of this solar system, that it previously existed near the throne of God, and when Adam fell the earth was brought into this solar system—

> This earth is our home, it was framed expressly for the habitation of those who are faithful to God, and who prove themselves worthy to inherit the earth when the Lord shall have sanctified, purified and glorified it and brought it back into his presence, from which it fell far into space…When the earth was framed and brought into existence and man was placed upon it, it was near the throne of our Father in heaven. And when man fell…the earth fell into space, and took up its abode in this planetary system, and the sun became our light. When the Lord said "Let there be light," there was light, for the earth was brought near the sun that it might reflect upon it so as to give us light by day, and the moon to give us light by night. This is the glory the earth came from, and when it is glorified it will return again unto the presence of the Father, and it will dwell there, and these intelligent beings that I am looking at, if they live worthy of it, will dwell upon this earth. (*Journal of Discourses,* Vol.17, p.144, Brigham Young, July 19, 1874)

So, without any knowledge of the conditions under which the earth existed prior to about 6000 years ago, there is no way for scientists to put a time line on its history. This is one of the interesting questions to which we may find the answers when we are no longer cumbered by the constraints of mortality.

—Gramps

WHEN A TEMPLE SEALING IS CANCELED, TO WHOM DO THE CHILDREN BELONG?

Dear Gramps,

I have recently gone through a divorce due to some actions my husband did that warrant excommunication from the church. My bishop has encouraged me to wait until such time as I have an opportunity to remarry in the temple to have the sealing between myself and my ex-husband canceled.

Even though I have concerns about him dying because of his lifestyle (thus making it harder to have the sealing canceled) I have decided to wait. The question I have is, Where does that leave my son who was born under the covenant if the sealing is canceled? Does he remain sealed to me?

Leah

Dear Leah,

It is good advice not to rush into the cancellation of an eternal sealing. We don't know what tomorrow may bring, and repentance and forgiveness are eternal principles. Many a person who has made serious mistakes in his life has subsequently repented, been forgiven, and gone on to accomplish great and marvelous things. The example of Alma the Younger comes quickly to mind. Not all, however, do return.

If your husband remains unworthy and the time comes that you would like to make an eternal alliance with someone else, that would be the time to consider a cancellation of the previous sealing.

The eternal family unit exists only for exalted beings in the celestial kingdom. The sealings of wives to husbands are valid only according to the faithfulness of each partner. If one partner violates the covenants, the promises made to the faithful partner remain in force, and a worthy partner will, in the Lord's own time and according to the desires of the faithful person, take the place of the erring one. The children will remain sealed only to the faithful partner who qualifies for the glory of exaltation in the celestial kingdom.

—Gramps

IS COFFEE FLAVORED ICE CREAM AGAINST THE WORD OF WISDOM?

Dear Gramps,

I am a convert, a member for about seven years now. I admit that before I was a member, I had coffee ice cream a lot. Since becoming a member, I gave up all things that are mentioned in the Word of Wisdom.

I have, however, seen members have coffee ice cream, telling me that it is not the same as having coffee. There have also been other members that told me to stay away from them. I have not been able to get a straight answer about coffee ice cream. I have been told that the ice creams have the flavor, but none of the ingredients that are found in coffee, is that true? I do

not want to go back to eating it if it is going against the Word of Wisdom. Can you please clarify where the lines are drawn? I await your answers. Thank you. Sincerely,
Nick in Provo

Dear Nick,

The Word of Wisdom is a formal document that has been accepted by members of the Church as a revelation from God and binding upon the membership. The proscriptions in the Word of Wisdom have been defined as tea, coffee, alcohol and tobacco. One is not violating the "Word of Wisdom" revelation *per se* when one partakes of things not mentioned in the revelation. For instance, it is not against the Word of Wisdom to take strychnine, because strychnine is not mentioned therein. However, everyone knows that strychnine "is not for the body, neither for the belly, and is not good for man."

There are those who excuse themselves in ingesting harmful materials simply because they are not mentioned in the Word of Wisdom. Such rationalization is only giving in to the bodily appetites and passions that we are enjoined to overcome. Rather than looking for acceptance by observing the actions of others, it would be well to rely on our own inspiration, as instructed by the Lord in D&C 46:7—

> *But ye are commanded in all things to ask of God, who giveth liberally; and that which the Spirit testifies unto you even so I would that ye should do in all holiness of heart, walking uprightly before me, considering the end of your salvation, doing all things with prayer and thanksgiving, that ye may not be seduced by evil spirits, or doctrines of devils, or the commandments of men; for some are of men, and others of devils.*

—Gramps

WHY MUST WE WAIT UNTIL AGE 16 BEFORE DATING?

Dear Gramps,
Why are we supposed to wait to date until we're 16? I'm 15 and I am mentally and emotionally mature enough to handle a relationship. My parents say it's because dating is a temptation to do evil, but I know I could handle it. Thank you,
Anna

Dear Anna,

I'm sure that you are a very mature young lady and very much in control of yourself. The 16th birthday is no magic number in terms of maturity. There is no doubt that some young women could easily handle themselves honorably in tempting situations even before that age. It is very necessary, nonetheless, for Church leaders to counsel young people against over-familiarity and to help prepare them for appropriate social behavior as they come into young adulthood. So standards of behavior must be established. It would be impossible to psychoanalyze each young person to determine his or her maturity level and commitment to high moral standards of behavior, and thus determine the appropriate age for that person to begin dating.

It is the same with the age of baptism. Children are not to be baptized before the age of accountability. Everyone knows that each child does not suddenly come into a degree of maturity on his or her eighth birthday, and thus immediately become accountable for his or her actions. But the Lord has established the 8th birthday as the minimum age that a child becomes accountable <u>before the Lord</u>. Thus the Church can act in an effective and appropriate manner in preparing children for baptism.

In like manner, a uniform minimum age has been established for dating, so that both group programs and individual guidance and counseling can objectively be carried out. This provides a wonderful opportunity for mature young people such as yourself to furnish the effective leadership of example to others who may not have the same level of maturity. As you demonstrate obedience to principal and encourage others to do the same, especially as you demonstrate by your obedience your ability to handle yourself in difficult social circumstances, your influence for good will be felt all around you, and you will be an instrument in our Father's hands to protect others from the ravages of sin.

—Gramps

DOES OUR BLOOD LITERALLY CHANGE TO THE BLOOD OF ISRAEL AT BAPTISM?

Dear Gramps,

A few days ago my bishop was teaching seminary and we were talking about the House of Israel. He made the comment that Brigham Young had said that when we are baptized into the church our blood changes to the blood of the House of Israel. That statement surprised me and when I asked if he meant it was a spiritual change, he said no, that it was literal. Is this true? And if it is where can I find the statement by Brigham Young? Also, if it is true, could you possibly clarify how this happens scientifically? Thank you,

    Gidgtmidgt

Dear Gidgtmidgt,

What do we mean by "the blood of the House of Israel"? The term "blood" in the context of genealogy signifies a literal descendency, as "of the same blood line." If genealogy could be traced as far back as Ephraim and Manasseh, it would be found that practically everyone could find some ancestral line leading to one of them. It has been said, for instance, that anyone who comes from England is related to everyone else who comes from England within thirty-three generations.

Occasionally we find from patriarchal blessings that one child of a family is descended from Ephraim and another from Manasseh. This situation could imply genetic differences that could have variations within the members of a given family, such as different eye color among siblings. Thus one child could be predominantly Ephraimitish and the other predominantly Manassehitish.

Abraham was given great promises with respect to his posterity.

> *And I will bless them that bless thee, and curse them that curse thee; and in thee (that is, in thy Priesthood) and in thy seed (that is, thy Priesthood), for I give unto thee a promise that this right shall continue in thee, and in thy seed after thee (that is to say, the literal seed, or the seed of the body) shall all the families of the earth be blessed, even with the blessings of the Gospel, which are the blessings of salvation, even of life eternal.* (Abraham 2:11)

Those who achieve the blessings of life eternal, or exaltation in the celestial kingdom, will live in a patriarchal order of priesthood, in an unbroken chain from Father Adam to the latest generation. Elder Bruce R. McConkie has stated that

> Those who shall hereafter rule and reign in eternity as exalted beings will form a patriarchal chain which will begin with Father Adam and spread out until every exalted person is linked in. Exaltation consists in the continuation of the family unit in eternity, and every family which so continues will find its proper place in the eternal organizational framework which the Almighty has ordained. None will be forgotten. Unworthy mortal links will be dropped in eternity, for there is no family in which all generations will attain exaltation; later generations of worthy families will be welded into the links formed by their ancestors who became worthy of a like exaltation with them. All those after the day of Abraham (of

whatever literal lineage they may be) who so live as to be worthy of a place in this great patriarchal chain will be welded into Abraham's lineage and shall rise up and bless him as their father. (Abr. 2:9-11; see also Bruce R. McConkie, *Mormon Doctrine,* p.558)

The Prophet Joseph Smith observed that
As the Holy Ghost falls upon one of the literal seed of Abraham, it is calm and serene…while the effect of the Holy Ghost upon a Gentile, is to purge out the old blood, and make him actually of the seed of Abraham. That man that has none of the blood of Abraham (naturally) must have a new creation by the Holy Ghost. *(Teachings of the Prophet Joseph Smith,* pp. 149-50)

So a person who is not of the House of Israel who lives worthily will be adopted into the patriarchal priesthood line, and will become, through the workings of the Holy Spirit, of that lineage in the same sense as if he had been born to it.
—Gramps

CAN YOU EXPLAIN THIS HUSBAND'S ACTIONS?

Dear Gramps,

Why would a divorced 37-year-old male in the military, with no children of his own, marry a 31-year-old divorced female with a child from her first marriage, and leave her behind two months later in the U.S. to serve a year duty tour in Korea?
Name Withheld

Dear Name Withheld,
1) He's a cad.
2) She's a cad.
3) Duty calls. Inevitable military assignment.
4) He volunteered for duty in order to get away.
5) He volunteered for duty because he loves his country more than his family.
6) His mother-in-law moved in.
7) Her mother-in-law moved in.
8) He can't stand the child.
9) She's not what he thought she would be.

10) He's not what she thought he would be, and she made
    life miserable for him.
—Gramps

How Did Eve Sin In Partaking Of The Forbidden Fruit?

Dear Gramps,

If it was necessary for Adam and Eve to eat of the fruit in order to become mortal and gain the power to procreate, why then was it considered a deception and transgression for Eve to choose to eat the fruit—or was there some other way that mortality could be accomplished besides eating the fruit?

Janet

Dear Janet,

In the first place God gave a commandment to Adam and Eve not to partake of the fruit of the Tree of Knowledge of Good and Evil.

> *But of the tree of the knowledge of good and evil, thou shalt not eat of it, nevertheless, thou mayest choose for thyself, for it is given unto thee; but, remember that I forbid it, for in the day thou eatest thereof thou shalt surely die.* (Moses 3:17)

Eve was in transgression because she listened to the temptings of Satan and disobeyed God's commandment, and by so doing she brought death into the world. Paul tell us that

> *And Adam was not deceived, but the woman being deceived was in the transgression.* (1 Timothy 2:14)

—Gramps

How Do I Cope With Hurtful Parents?

Dear Gramps,

My father and mother are from Germany. Many children in Germany are raised in the old tradition of silence. My father never speaks to me unless I directly approach him, and my mother conveys messages but is pretty much a hands-off, and mouth-shut mother. I was never told not to do things that are contrary to moral and ethical practices. Now how was I expected to know those things were wrong if my parents didn't tell me? Well,

I've stayed alive somehow, and my parents are getting elderly. At family gatherings my father is a non-stop talker to my spouse but when I walk into a room where he is alone, he "pretends" to be asleep. Lately he has made several very hurtful comments about some money I owe him even though all the arrangements have been made to pay him back. I no longer want to go home; I always leave in tears. I am the only child that he still treats this way, and I'm the only Latter-day Saint.

Lost in Michigan

Dear Lost in Michigan,

Do you think that there is any connection between your being a Latter-day Saint and the way your parents treat you? Those who have other firm religious beliefs or who have been taught false and unsavory information about The Church of Jesus Christ of Latter-day Saints may be highly opposed to their daughter joining a group that they feel is not right. Their opposition to such moves, stemming from a position of ignorance or false information, comes because the parent loves the child and does not want anything bad to happen to him or her. That love may often be expressed as hatred—not hatred for the individual, but hatred for the concepts that the individual has espoused.

Perhaps there are other reasons why your parents may be uncomfortable with who you are or what you do. It is sometimes difficult to find out opinions that are held with a degree of emotion. You could ask them if they have any negative feelings toward you, and what they would like you to do in order for their feelings to change. If that course is not appropriate you might ask your brothers and sisters. If that is not a viable option, it would probably be well to treat them with deference and respect and honor them in every way that you can. Eventually such behavior, especially when it is not expected, can have very beneficial effects on healing a relationship.

You mention that your parents never instructed you in moral and ethical values, and you seem to hold some resentment because of that. It is sometimes very difficult for people to express themselves about sensitive issues. Even though you may not have had such instruction, I imagine that you could figure out for yourself without much difficulty what was right and what was wrong. The Spirit of Christ, given to every creature, allows us to understand the difference between right and wrong. It is sometimes called the conscience. Moroni encourages us to develop the sensitivity to recognize and utilize this great gift.

> *Wherefore, I beseech of you, brethren, that ye should search diligently in the light of Christ that ye may know good from evil; and if ye will lay hold upon every good thing, and condemn it not, ye certainly will be a child of Christ.* (Moroni 7:19)

—Gramps

SHOULD WE CELEBRATE HALLOWEEN?

Dear Gramps

I am a convert, and even before I was a member, I thought that celebrating Halloween (or All Hallows Eve), was helping Satan have a sort of "Christmas." What does the prophet have to say on this matter?

Barbara

Dear Barbara,

Halloween, or All Saints Even, is celebrated on the evening preceding All Saints Day. By most accounts, the Halloween tradition dates back to the 7th century (or earlier). A Celtic religious order, the Druids, were found in Britain, France and Ireland. October 31st, called Samhain, was officially the end of their summer. All the crops were harvested, and preparations were made for the upcoming winter.

It was also on this day, more than any other, that they believed all the disembodied spirits came back to try to possess the living. The townspeople dressed up in strange garb, fires were extinguished in the homes to make them inhospitable, and all efforts were made in order to draw these spirits away from the town.

As Christianity spread to these areas, the Catholic Church, in an attempt to convert them, tried to placate the pagans by proclaiming November 1st as All Saints Day or All Hallows Day to honor the saints and martyrs yet to be sanctified. Since this didn't cover normal folk, they later named November 2nd as All Souls Day. However it is October 31, the night before All Saints Day (all Hallows Eve) that later became known as 'Halloween'.

The jack o'lantern is based on an old Irish legend about the drunk, Jack, who tricked Satan into a tree to throw down some fruit. Once he was in the tree, Jack carved a cross in the trunk, and only allowed Satan down after he swore not to claim Jack's soul after he died.

When Jack died, he was denied heaven because of his evil ways, and Satan would not take him because of his promise (and anger at being tricked). Instead, the devil threw Jack an ember to light his way through the eternal darkness he now found himself in. Jack put the ember in a carved turnip to act as a lantern. The turnip was eventually replaced with the traditional pumpkin, as they're more readily available.

There are several different beliefs about the origins of Trick or Treat. One cited most often is the 9th-century practice in England called "souling". On All Souls Day, Christians would go from village to village begging for "soul cakes" (square pieces of currant bread). In return for the cakes, the beggars would promise to say prayers for the dead relatives of the donors.

The origins of Halloween have been all but forgotten, and only the ritualistic form is left, having been converted into a national holiday. As far as I know, the Church has made no official statements with respect to national holidays. However, with respect to the observance of Halloween, or in any other social event, church members are discouraged from wearing masks. The wearing of a mask hiding the identity of the individual would tend to give license to inappropriate behavior.

—Gramps

WHY DOES THE BOOK OF MORMON USE THE GREEK TRANSLATION FOR THE NAME OF THE SAVIOR RATHER THAN THE HEBREW NAME?

Dear Gramps,
I have read that the name Jesus Christ is a Greek translation of his Hebrew name. If that is true, why then would the Book of Mormon refer to Him as Christ and to the church as Christians when Greek would not have been used by the Nephites?
Robyn

Dear Robyn,
The name Jesus Christ is the English translation of the Greek Iesous Christos. But Iesous is the Greek translation of the Hebrew Yeshua—the English translation of which is Joshua. So the Savior was probably called Yeshua by his contemporaries. And had we received the New Testament as a translation from the Hebrew rather than from the Greek, the Savior would probably have been known to us as Joshua the Messiah.

Nephi and his contemporaries spoke Hebrew, but they recorded their sacred scriptures in Egyptian. So in the plates of the Book of Mormon the inscription for the words "Jesus Christ" was undoubtedly the Egyptian equivalent of Joshua the Messiah.

When Joseph Smith translated the records into English, he very logically used the English translation of the proper names that were written on the plates. For instance, the name, Melchizedek, which is the English translation of Malkiy-Tsedeq, is mentioned in the Book of Mormon. If the Hebrew word, rather than its English translation, were used, very few people would know who was being referred to.

—Gramps

How Did Joseph Smith Receive Revelation?

Dear Gramps,

How did Joseph Smith receive revelation from the Lord? Was he alone and wrote what was told him from memory afterward, or was there a scribe in attendance at the time of each revelation? Or was there some other method by which Joseph was able to put to paper what he was commanded to reveal to us? Thank you,

Richard

Dear Richard,

Joseph Smith often employed scribes to write the revelations that he received, in some cases as they were being received. Here is an interesting account of one such occurrence recorded by Howard Coray, one of Joseph's clerks:

> One morning, I went as usual, into the office to go to work: I found Joseph sitting on one side of a table and Robert B. Thompson on the opposite side, and the understanding I got was that they were examining or hunting in the manuscript of the new translation of the Bible for something on Priesthood, which Joseph wished to present, or have read to the people the next Conference: Well, they could not find what they wanted and Joseph said to Thompson "put the manuscript to one side, and take some paper and I will tell you what to write." Bro. Thompson took some foolscap paper that was at his elbow and made himself ready for the business. I was seated probably 6 or 8 feet on Joseph's left side, so that I could look almost squarely into Joseph's left eye—I mean the side of his eye. Well, the Spirit of God descended upon him, and a measure of it upon me, insomuch that I could fully realize that God, or the Holy Ghost, was talking through him. I never, neither before or since, have felt as I did on that

occasion. I felt so small and humble I could have freely kissed his feet."
(Special Collections, Brigham Young University, p. 51)

On other occasions, the revelations were written many years after having been received, such as D&C 132, which was recorded on 12 July 1843.
However, this revelation was received by the prophet probably sometime in
1831.

D&C Section 76 is the record of a vision that was seen by Joseph and
Sidney Rigdon at the home of Father Johnson in Hyrum, Ohio, in the presence of about a dozen persons. Philo Dibble, who was among those present,
recorded the following account:.

> Joseph would, at intervals, say: "What do I see?" Then he would
> relate what he had seen or what he was looking at. Then Sidney replied,
> "I see the same." Presently Sidney would say, "What do I see?" and would
> repeat what he had seen or was seeing, and Joseph would reply, "I see the
> same." This manner of conversation was repeated at short intervals to the
> end of the vision, and during the whole time not a word was spoken by
> any other person. Not a sound nor motion made by anyone but Joseph and
> Sidney, and it seemed to me that they never moved a joint or limb during
> the time I was there, which I think was over an hour, and to the end of
> the vision. Joseph sat firmly and calmly all the time in the midst of a
> magnificent glory, but Sidney sat limp and pale, apparently as limber as a
> rag, observing which Joseph remarked, smilingly, "Sidney is not used to
> it as I am." (*The Juvenile Instructor*, May 15, 1892, pp. 303, 304)

Of significance is the fact that Joseph Smith apparently did not write
Section 76. The commandment to write the vision was given in verse 28,

> *And while we were yet in the Spirit, the Lord commanded us that we
> should write the vision.*

Ivan J. Barrett reports in his book titled *Joseph Smith and the
Restoration*, p. 204, that Joseph requested Sidney Rigdon to write the
vision, and that he stayed up the entire night following the vision to put it
in written form.

Some revelations were received by the prophet by means of the Urim
and Thummim. See, for example, D&C 7. At other times angelic messen-
gers appeared to him to deliver the word of God. See, for example, D&C
13 and 110.

So the prophet was not restricted to any one means of receiving the
word of the Lord. President Wilford Woodruff had this to say on the subject:

> What is revelation? It is the inspiration of the Holy Ghost to man.
> Joseph Smith said to Brother John Taylor in his day: "Brother Taylor, you

watch the impression of the Spirit of God; you watch the whisperings of Spirit to you; you carry them out in your life, and it will become a principle of revelation in you, and you will know and understand this spirit and power." This is the key, the foundation stone of all revelation. Joseph Smith was full of revelation. He could translate anything given to him of God. He could receive revelation without the Urim and Thummim. Many of the principal revelations contained in the Doctrine and Covenants were received without the use of the Urim and Thummim. They were given to him by the inspiration of Almighty God. In my own experience I have endeavored to get acquainted with that Spirit, and to learn its operations. I have many times had that Spirit manifested to me, and if I had not followed its whisperings to me, I should have been in my grave long ago, with many of my companions. (*The Discourses of Wilford Woodruff*, pp. 45-46)

—Gramps

To Whom Are Children Of Divorced Parents Sealed?

Dear Gramps,

My wife is not sealed to her parents. Both are remarried and have now joined the church. I am wondering who is she sealed to? Her father and stepmother, her mother and stepfather, or her father and mother?

Doug

Dear Doug,

Your wife was apparently not sealed to her natural parents since they didn't belong to the church until after they were divorced and remarried, so it doesn't look like she's sealed to anybody. If a person is born under the covenant, i.e., if the parents were sealed together before the child was born, then that child is sealed to its natural parents. If children are not born under the covenant, they must be sealed to their parents in the temple. If children are old enough to be endowed, they must be endowed before being sealed to their parents. Of course, all must be worthy of a temple recommend.

If your wife's parents were divorced and then married other partners and both couples joined the church and then were sealed to each other, any children that any of them had could be sealed to either one of their natural parents and spouse according to the desires of all concerned.

The sealings performed in the temples are all conditional upon the worthiness of the participants. We must remain true and faithful to all our covenants in order to be worthy to inherit the celestial kingdom and maintain the family relationships that were sealed on earth.

—Gramps

SHOULD BOTH WIVES—THE LIVING AND THE DECEASED—BE SEALED TO THEIR HUSBAND ON THE SAME DAY?

Dear Gramps,

My husband and I are being sealed next month. Some of his children are asking that we take this opportunity to also seal him to their mother, from whom he was divorced before her death many years ago, so that they may then be sealed to their parents. We do not want to do so at this time, but are open to arranging it sometime in the future. They are convinced it is necessary to be sealed to their parents in order to reach their highest exaltation. If that is true, we will accommodate them with a happy heart. If that is not true, how do we say no in the kindest way? We feel this is "our" special time.

Sister Heighton

Dear Sister Heighton,

To achieve exaltation in the celestial kingdom it is necessary to live according to the covenants we make in the temple. If a couple are sealed together, and are not sealed to their parents during their mortal probation, that will not prevent them from realizing all their promised blessings in eternity. All the necessary ancestral linkage will be taken care of in its appropriate time.

There are some unanswered questions that would affect your circumstance. Was the children's mother a member of the church? If a member, had she been sealed to their father before she passed away? Another important question is whether or not your husband would want to be sealed to his first wife. These are the prime considerations.

Further, if all was in order, and it were appropriate to have the children sealed to their natural parents, it would seem to me not at all appropriate to complicate your sealing with the sealing of your husband to someone else at the same time. I think that with all the feelings that are naturally involved in such circumstances that it would at the very least be considerate of the children to have themselves sealed to their parents on a different occasion.

—Gramps

WHY SHOULD TAROT CARD READINGS BE AVOIDED?

Dear Gramps,

My 20-year-old daughter recently got a "tarot card" reading. There is a young woman in her student ward that does these readings "just for fun!" My daughter was saying that since this girl is LDS she does a "gospel" take on the readings of the tarot card.

First of all, I am a bit leery of these types of things, and have cautioned her to be very careful. I have to admit that I read my horoscope on occasion, only to get a good chuckle out of them. BUT, in this case, she is seeing that some of the things this girl is saying are true in her case! She was struggling with a decision, had told no one except me, and then the tarot cards said that she was struggling with a certain decision.

I am frightened of these types of things. I know that Ouija boards are supposed to be avoided at all costs. What about tarot cards, and if they ARE to be avoided, give me a good valid reason to tell her to stay away from them. I have tried the old standard reasoning of "Mom just doesn't have a good feeling about it!" Thank you very much,

This Mom

Dear Mom,

Tarot cards, Ouija boards, tea leaves, and all other mechanisms that may be used for contacting the spirits of departed persons fall in the same class. They are frequently used to bilk the innocent, credulous, curious and unwary of their money by pretending to make contact with the dead.

I would imagine that not everyone, however, is a charlatan. But there is no doubt that if any departed spirits attempt to communicate with the living through such media, they do so under the influence of the adversary, and not under the influence of the Lord. The information given out by such "mediums" can never be trusted. Either the medium is a fraud or is a dupe of satanic influences. In either case, some true things could be said which serve to deceive the gullible. The fraudulent mediums often speak in such generalities that what they say may fit entire classes of people. In addition, in serious cases, they may even find out specific information about some person and pass it on as having come from the spirit world.

I think that your daughter would be well advised to leave such information entirely alone, and rely instead on the Holy Spirit for guidance and direction in her life.

—Gramps

CAN YOU TELL ME THE CHURCH'S DOCTRINE ABOUT MISCARRIAGES AND STILLBIRTHS?

Dear Gramps,
What is the doctrine about miscarriage and stillbirth? I am interested in your opinion. Thank you,
Paula

Dear Paula,
As you will read below, we do not have specific revelation recorded in the scriptures concerning when the spirit enters the body. However, Elder Bruce R. McConkie has written on the subject and has cited the opinions of the First Presidency consisting of Joseph F. Smith, John R. Winder, and Anthon H. Lund, and also the opinion of Brigham Young. Coming from the prophets, these could be considered as authoritative opinions. I think they would not be classed as doctrine, however.

> When the fetus is born dead, it is said to be a stillbirth. Such an occurrence gives rise to anxiety on the part of mothers, in particular, as to whether the stillborn baby had in fact become a living soul, whether the partially or nearly formed body had become the home of a pre-existent spirit, and whether such a body will be resurrected. These are matters not clearly answered in the revelation so far available for the guidance of the saints in this dispensation. No doubt such things were plainly set forth in those past dispensations when more of the doctrines of salvation were known and taught than have been revealed so far to us.

> That masterful document on the origin of man by the First Presidency of the Church (Joseph F. Smith, John R. Winder, and Anthon H. Lund) appears to bear out the concept that the eternal spirit enters the body prior to a normal birth, and therefore that stillborn children will be resurrected. It states: "The body of man enters upon its career as a tiny germ or embryo, which becomes an infant, quickened at a certain stage by the spirit whose tabernacle it is, and the child, after being born, develops into a man." (*Man: His Origin and Destiny,* p. 354)

This interpretation is in harmony with the general knowledge we have of the mercy and justice of that Infinite Being in whose divine economy nothing is ever lost. It would appear that we can look forward with hope and anticipation for the resurrection of stillborn children.

> President Brigham Young taught that "when the mother feels life come to her infant, it is the spirit entering the body preparatory to the immortal existence," and President Joseph Fielding Smith gave it as his opinion "that these little ones will receive a resurrection and then belong to us." "Stillborn children should not be reported nor recorded as births

and deaths on the records of the Church," he said, "but it is suggested that parents record in their own family records a name of each such stillborn child." (*Doctrines of Salvation,* vol. 2, pp. 280-281; see also Bruce R. McConkie, *Mormon Doctrine,* p.768)

—Gramps

DO ALL CELESTIAL MARRIAGES INVOLVE POLYGAMY?

Dear Gramps,

My question concerns polygamy. I have heard that all celestial marriages will involve polygamy in the celestial kingdom. I have also heard that this is not the case or that it will be so for only some people. What is the real answer? Will all of us who make it into the celestial kingdom and are married be involved in polygamy?

Robyn

Dear Robyn,

We know, of course, that no polygamous marriages have been contracted in the kingdom for well over 100 years, and even in the early days, plural marriage was practiced by only a few who were called upon to do so, or who received permission to do so. I know of no doctrine that declares that plural marriage is a requirement for exaltation.

—Gramps

WAS JESUS MARRIED?

Dear Gramps,

Jesus was baptized and, in order to return to His Father and enter the celestial kingdom, did He have to have an earthly marriage or would He be the only one in the celestial kingdom unmarried? Could He have been married before leaving for His mission? In order for us to enter the celestial kingdom we have to be a pair—husband and wife, priest and priestess, kings and queens. This has been asked of me by my non-Mormon friends who I have talked with about the gospel. I have explained that there must be a husband and a wife to enter the celestial kingdom and we have sealings of marriages for our ancestors (I was explaining the reasons for the

new Boston Temple) which take place in the temple. What do I answer to my friends when they ask about Christ and if He was married?
   Janet

Dear Janet,
   There is no place in the scriptures that <u>explicitly</u> states that the Savior was married. However, there is also no place in the scriptures that indicates that He was not married. Although He was the only person to live on the earth without sin, He nevertheless subjected himself to the ordinance of baptism, which is administered for the remission of sins. Although He did not need to be baptized for the remission of sins, He instructed John to perform the ordinance *for thus it becometh us to fulfill all righteousness*. The Savior demonstrated that He was not above the law, and subjected Himself to all the laws and ordinances of the gospel, and thus became the exemplar of obedience to the Father.
   Those who live in accordance with the covenants made at baptism are worthy to inherit the celestial kingdom. To achieve exaltation in the celestial kingdom, it is necessary to enter into the new and everlasting covenant of marriage. It would be against all logic and reason to suppose that the Savior would not subject himself to the essential ordinance for exaltation in the celestial kingdom, having complied with the essential ordinance to enter the celestial kingdom.
   Several of the brethren have stated the Jesus was married, and have expressed the opinion that He was the bridegroom at the wedding in Cana where He performed his first recorded miracle by changing water into wine to be used at the wedding feast. B. H. Roberts quotes Orson Hyde as follows:

> We say it was Jesus Christ who was married (at Cana) to the Marys and Martha, whereby he could see his seed before he was crucified. — Apostle Orson Hyde, *Journal of Discourses*, Volume II. (B.H. Roberts, *Defense of the Faith and the Saints,* Vol.2, p. 272)

In another reference, Orson Hyde recorded the following:

> It will be borne in mind that once on a time, there was a marriage in Cana of Galilee; and on a careful reading of that transaction, it will be discovered that no less a person than Jesus Christ was married on that occasion. (*Journal of Discourses*, Vol.4, p.259, Orson Hyde)

—Gramps

WHERE DID ADAM AND EVE COME FROM?

Gramps,
Would you please clarify the origins of Adam and Eve? Were they trans-
planted here? Were their physical bodies created from the elements of this
earth? Were the elements of this earth also immortal and when they fell, did
it fall also? Anything else you would like to expand on this subject is appre-
ciated.
Spudgam

Dear Spudgam,
The biblical account of the creation of Adam and Eve is highly alle-
gorical. The actual account of their origin is completely logical and highly
pleasing and satisfying to the rational mind. Brigham Young explained it as
follows:

> Though we have it in history that our father Adam was made of the
> dust of this earth, and that he knew nothing about his God previous to
> being made here, yet it is not so; and when we learn the truth we shall see
> and understand that he helped to make this world, and was the chief man-
> ager in that operation.
>
> He was the person who brought the animals and the seeds from other
> planets to this world, and brought a wife with him and stayed here. You
> may read and believe what you please as to what is found written in the
> Bible. Adam was made from the dust of an earth, but not from the dust of
> this earth. He was made as you and I are made, and no person was ever
> made upon any other principle. (*Journal of Discourses*, Vol.3, p.319)

When Adam and Eve came to this earth, it was a terrestrial sphere and
Adam and Eve were terrestrial beings. It is logical to assume that they were
born on a terrestrial world, and that the flora and fauna that exist on this
earth are similar to that on the world that Adam came from.

The terrestrial state of this earth lasted until Adam and Eve partook of
the fruit of the Tree of Knowledge of Good and Evil. As a consequence of
that act, the earth and all its inhabitants were changed to a telestial condition. That transition took place around 4,000 B.C. We talk of the seven
thousand years of the earth's temporal existence. (D&C 77:6) Brigham
Young reveals some fascinating information about the earth's transition
from its terrestrial to its telestial state:

> This earth is our home, it was framed expressly for the habitation of
> those who are faithful to God, and who prove themselves worthy to inherit
> the earth when the Lord shall have sanctified, purified and glorified it and
> brought it back into his presence, from which it fell far into space…when
> the earth was framed and brought into existence and man was placed upon

it, it was near the throne of our Father in Heaven. And when man fell…the earth fell into space, and took up its abode in this planetary system, and the sun became our light. When the Lord said— 'Let there be light,' there was light, for the earth was brought near the sun that it might reflect upon it so as to give us light by day, and the moon to give us light by night. This is the glory the earth came from, and when it is glorified it will return again unto the presence of the Father, and it will dwell there, and these intelligent beings that I am looking at, if they live worthy of it, will dwell upon this earth. (*Journal of Discourses*, Vol.17, p.144)

This is a surprising doctrine to many—that the earth is a newcomer to the solar system. But as we look at all the new information about the solar planets revealed by the recent space probes, it is not all that surprising. This earth is vastly different from all the other planets. There is also some compelling information that indicates that the earth is not the newest member of our planetary system. Dr. Immanuel Velikofsky, in his book, *Worlds in Collision,* develops compelling evidence that Venus was a comet that was captured by the sun at about 1500 A.D.

The earth itself is indeed a living being, with intelligence and volition. The earth obeys all the laws required of celestial beings and will inherit a celestial glory. We read in D&C 88:18-20 that

it must needs be sanctified from all unrighteousness, that it may be prepared for the celestial glory, For after it hath filled the measure of its creation, it shall be crowned with glory, even with the presence of God the Father;

That bodies who are of the celestial kingdom may possess it forever and ever; for, for this intent was it made and created, and for this intent are they sanctified.

Orson F. Whitney has written that

The earth, which is a living creature, will be exalted to shine among the stars of God as a celestial body, that beings of a celestial order may inherit it for ever and for ever. Says he: "All kingdoms have a law given," then if this earth is to become a celestial kingdom, we must obey the law of the celestial kingdom, if we desire to inherit it. For this earth is our heaven, and we will return to it if we are worthy of an inheritance on its surface. (*Collected Discourses*, Vol.1)

—Gramps

WERE THERE PRE-COLUMBIAN
HORSES IN AMERICA?

Dear Gramps,

The Book of Mormon states that the Nephites and Jaredites had horses (1 Ne. 18:25; 2 Ne. 12:7; Enos 1:21; Alma 18:9-12; 3 Ne. 3:22, 21:14; Ether 9:19) and elephants. (Ether 9:19) If they did, why did the Indians (Lamanites) not know about horses when the explorers came to the new world? And do you know if there is any archaeological evidence that there were horses and elephants on the American continent when the Jaredites and Nephites were around? Thanks Gramps,

Gidgt

Dear Gidgt,

It is not true that the Lamanites knew nothing of the horse when the Spaniards arrived. It is true that the Spaniards found no horses in Mexico, Central America and Peru, and from that deduced that there were no horses on the American continent. However, Sir Francis Drake, visiting the west coast of North America, saw "large bands of wild horses," as quoted below:

> So far as the nonexistence of the horse in ancient America is concerned, the question has forever been set at rest by the discovery of the remains of this animal all over the land; and though Cortez and his followers saw none alive, yet Admiral Sir Francis Drake did see large bands of wild horses on the Oregon Coast in 1579, far too early for any to have escaped from the Spaniards, grown wild, and traveled so vast a distance. (Reynolds and Sjodahl, *Commentary on the Book of Mormon,* Vol. 6, p.236)

There has been work performed at Gypsum Cave and other locations "where mammoth, mastodon, camel and horse are associated with man, and there is a map showing twenty-three places where extinct animals have been associated with man in the United States." (M.R. Harrington, Gypsum Cave, Nevada, Southwest Museum Papers, No. 8, 37)

I have observed the skeletons of prehistoric horses in a museum of natural history in Buenos Aires, Argentina, that were discovered in Argentina by Charles Darwin (1809-1882). I could tell no difference from the skeletons of modern horses except for one particular. The bone extending over the nose of the modern horse is about four inches long after it separates from the rest of the skull; however, on those pre-historic horses that bone was about 10 inches long.

Concerning elephants: the elephant is a close relative to the wooly mammoth and the mastodon—both have tusks and trunks and are about the same size as elephants. Again, I have seen the remains of a wooly mammoth that is currently being excavated in Nebraska. Although it is not yet on public display, it is being prepared by the Dawson County Historical Society in Lexington, Nebraska. The entire skull (with tusks) has been excavated and transported to the museum.

> The Mastodon…is known to have survived into the historical period. According to Mr. M. R. Harrison, curator of the Los Angeles Museum, the earliest inhabitants of California, the "Folsom" people, hunted both bisons and mammoths, the latter being also known as extinct elephants. Obsidian spearheads and knives, we are informed, have been found among bones of those extinct animals on the shores of a pond in Clear Lake Park, where the people mentioned seem to have had a favorite camp. (Reynolds and Sjodahl, *Commentary on the Book of Mormon,* Vol. 6, p.144)

The Folsom people apparently pre-dated the Nephite and Jaredite cultures, but evidence shows that the horse and 'elephant' were native to the American Continent before the advent of the Book of Mormon cultures, rather than being introduced by Europeans in the 1500's.

—Gramps

WILL WE RECOGNIZE ONE ANOTHER IN THE AFTERLIFE?

Dear Gramps,

I have a dear friend who is widowed and lives alone. He is a retired air traffic controller in Tuscaloosa, AL. He is 88 years old and retains all his faculties. He is not a member of the Church. His wife suffered for five years before she passed away. He cared for her by himself all that time. He has asked me several times what I think about her present state, and if he will know her in the spirit world. I have been sealed to my wife in the temple, and know the answers to his questions. However, I have trouble explaining it to him. I wonder if you would answer these questions for him. His name is Wiley. My best to you. I enjoy what you are doing.

Tom

Dear Wiley,

Your friend, Tom, has mentioned to me the recent loss of your wife, after what appears to be a lifetime together. He suggested that I might be able to shed a little light on some of the concerns we have about our loved ones who depart this life. Although my wife and I are still together after 50 years of marriage, we did lose a daughter four years ago, who passed away suddenly at age 33, so we may have some indication of the feelings and concerns that you may have with respect to your own family.

I have spent my life as a member of the Church of Jesus Christ of Latter-day Saints, and so adhere to their teachings and philosophy concerning the things of eternity. One of the distinctive characteristics of The Church of Jesus Christ of Latter-day Saints is that it has been presided over since its organization in 1830 by men who have been called of God as His prophets to the people. They receive continuing revelations from God for the benefit of man in our times, and bear the same relationship to Him as did the prophets of old. To explain to you what we know about the afterlife, I will probably quote from some of their revelations, but whatever I say will have been garnered from what God has revealed to them.

First, let me say that the life of the body in mortality is sustained by the spirit that inhabits the body. The spirit is an actual person, (the real us) comprised of spiritual material. Our spirits existed before we were born into mortality as begotten children of our Father in Heaven. That statement makes reasonable the scripture found in John 9:1-3

As Jesus passed by, he saw a man which was blind from his birth. And his disciples asked him, saying, Master, who did sin, this man, or his parents, that he was born blind? Jesus answered, Neither hath this man sinned, nor his parents: but that the works of God should be made manifest in him.

His disciples understood that the man lived before his birth and in his pre-mortal state was capable of sinning.

Before birth we lived with our Father in Heaven. We had in that realm our individual personalities, appearances, likes and dislikes; and we were free to choose what we would do, as much as we are free in mortality to do so. The spirit enters the mortal body at birth, giving it independent life.

Brigham Young, the second president of the Church, had this to say on the subject:

There is not a person here today but what is a son or a daughter of that Being. In the spirit world their spirits were first begotten and brought forth, and they lived there with their parents for ages before they came here. This, perhaps, is hard for many to believe, but it is the greatest nonsense in the world not to believe it. If you do not believe it, cease to call him Father; and when you pray, pray to some other character. (*Discourses of Brigham Young*, p. 50)

At death the spirit leaves the body. In fact, that is the definition of death. Some people, horribly mangled in terrible accidents, continue to live— because the spirit still resides in the body. Others, in seemingly good health, pass away in an instant, simply because the spirit, having been called home by the Father, leaves the body. And without that central, guiding intelligence, the body, inanimate, begins to decay and decompose.

When the spirit leaves the body, where does it go? Again, Brigham Young sheds specific light on the subject:

> When you lay down this tabernacle, where are you going? Into the spiritual world. Are you going into Abraham's bosom? No, not anywhere nigh there but into the spirit world. Where is the spirit world? It is right here. Do the good and evil spirits go together? Yes, they do. Do they both inhabit one kingdom? Yes, they do. Do they go to the sun? No. Do they go beyond the boundaries of the organized earth? No, they do not. They are brought forth upon this earth, for the express purpose of inhabiting it to all eternity. Where else are you going? Nowhere else, only as you may be permitted. (*Discourses of Brigham Young*, p. 376)

Although we cannot see into the spirit world, it is all around us. This is not unusual; the air is all around us, and we cannot see it. The prophet Joseph Smith, speaking at the funeral of James Adams, said:

> Brother Adams has gone to open up a more effectual door for the dead. The spirits of the just are exalted to a greater and more glorious work; hence they are blessed in their departure to the world of spirits. Enveloped in flaming fire, they are not far from us, and know and understand our thoughts, feelings, and motions, and are often pained therewith. (*Teachings of the Prophet Joseph Smith*, Section Six 1843-44, p. 325)

So, the fact is that life goes on! Death is no great thing. It is like taking off a cloak and walking through a door. At death we do not cease to exist; we do not become someone else. The process of death is no great thing to those who experience it, except that we enter a realm of great wonder and beauty, and gain great abilities that were denied us when clothed upon with our mortal tabernacles. Again, Brigham Young had the following to say about conditions in the spirit world:

> We shall turn round and look upon it [the valley of death] and think, when we have crossed it, why this is the greatest advantage of my whole existence, for I have passed from a state of sorrow, grief, mourning, woe, misery, pain, anguish and disappointment into a state of existence, where I can enjoy life to the fullest extent as far as that can be done without a body. My spirit is set free, I thirst no more, I want to sleep no more, I hunger no more, I tire no more, I run, I walk, I labor, I go, I come, I do this, I do that, whatever is required of me, nothing like pain or weariness,

I am full of life, full of vigor, and I enjoy the presence of my heavenly Father. (Funeral sermon 14th Ward, July 1874)

So, if we knew the truth, we should be happy for those who depart this life. Sorrow at the passing of a loved one is indeed appropriate, but it should be the sorrow that we normally feel by the temporary separation of association and companionship.

There is much more that could be said on this subject. What are the spirits doing in the post-mortal spirit world? What is the future from that vantage point to be like? Much detail related to these subjects is found in Doctrine & Covenants, Section 138. If interested, you might ask your friend, Tom, to go over this section with you. He could explain what it means and I'm sure could answer questions that would come to your mind.

—Gramps

DID GOD EVER INTEND MAN TO FLY?

Dear Gramps,

I've been troubled for a long time about whether God intended for man to fly. If He intended it, why weren't we born with wings, like a butterfly?

My second question is more pressing, and less theological— do I keep the stick way back on landing, or just a little ways, and do I do it down close, or up a little? Please answer, because I'm going to go fly my airplane pretty quick. Just as soon as I get your answer, probably. Maybe, in fact, I can't wait for your answer.

23 Skidoo

Dear Skidoo,

There is no doubt that God did not intend for man to fly. Man is endowed with none of the qualities essential for flight. Birds probably have a pretty good idea of whether the horizon is horizontal or whether it's off at some skewed angle, the discovery of which has given more than one pilot a near heart attack. Also, swallows don't need a GPS or a calendar to return to San Juan Capistrano from some place in South America on the same day each year. In addition, birds, not being IFR qualified, seem to have enough sense to fly clear of clouds, a bit of wisdom denied to many pilots.

Flying is one of the forbidden fruits with which mankind is tempted. We all remember as children lying on our backs on the green lawn on a warm summer afternoon and gazing in awe at the hawks circling effortlessly and silently overhead, wishing with all our hearts that we could do the same. If God wanted man to fly He would have provided him with airline tickets.

Now, concerning your second question. Forget the stick! Well, don't actually forget it; it does come in handy from time to time. But there is a general misconception in the field of aviation that pulling back on the stick makes the airplane go up and pushing forward on the stick makes it go down. Wrong! If one is flying straight and level with the aircraft trimmed for level flight, such that the controls only need to be caressed now and then to correct for bumps in the road, and one pulls back on the stick, the aircraft will not climb, it will merely slow up. If instead, one pushes the stick forward, the aircraft will not begin to descend, but will merely pick up speed, remaining at the same altitude. If, in the trimmed condition, one wishes to gain altitude, one merely advances the throttle. With the increased power, the aircraft will not pick up speed but will begin to climb. If one wishes to descend, merely retard the throttle, and the plane will not slow down, but will begin to descend at the same speed. So, contrary to popular opinion, the stick controls the speed and the throttle controls the altitude.

To land an airplane, on the downwind leg, reduce power and trim the airplane so with neutral controls the plane is descending at the desired rate. Then on final approach, minor adjustments to the throttle will make the plane go up or down to bring it in contact with the runway at the desired spot. There are those bird-like aviators who can land a plane without touching the stick. I confess that I have never met any of them, but I keep hearing that they are around. Happy flying.

—Gramps

From Which Parent Does A Child Receive His Or Her Lineage?

Dear Gramps,
Can you tell me from which parent does a child receive his or her lineage, particularly if the parents are from different tribes? Thanks,
Jeff

Dear Jeff,
We all receive our lineage from both parents. For instance, if your father was a Scotsman and your mother a German, you would have both

Scottish and German ancestry. Here are a couple of quotes from presidents Brigham Young and Joseph Fielding Smith on the subject:

> Israel is dispersed among all the nations of the earth; the blood of Ephraim is mixed with the blood of all the earth. Abraham's seed is mingled with the rebellious seed through the whole world of mankind. (*Discourses of Brigham Young*, p.437)

> Therefore, through the scattering of Israel among the nations, the blood of Israel was mixed with the Gentile nations, fulfilling the promise made to Abraham. Most of the members of the Church, although they are designated as descendants of Abraham, through Israel, also have in their veins Gentile blood. This is to say, no one is a direct descendant through Ephraim through each generation, or through Manasseh or any other one of the sons of Jacob, without having acquired the blood of some other tribe in Israel in that descent. (Joseph Fielding Smith, *Answers to Gospel Questions*, Vol. 3, p. 62)

Through patriarchal blessings it is occasionally found that one child in a family is of the blood of Ephraim and another child of the blood of another of the twelve tribes of Israel. That doesn't mean that either child has none of the blood of the other tribe, but that he is an heir of the blessings pertaining to that tribe, and through that tribe an heir to the blessings of father Abraham. However, the inheritance of those blessings to which he is heir depends upon his faithfulness in obeying the principles of the gospel.

—Gramps

HOW DO YOU EXPLAIN THE POWER OF THE PRIESTHOOD TO NON-MEMBERS?

Dear Gramps,

I have a question that I wish someone could answer satisfactorily. I have asked this question since I was sixteen. I am the only member of the church on my mother's side. I often get the heat from them for belonging to a cult, but we also exchange our beliefs. The one thing I am having a hard time explaining to them is the power of the priesthood. I tell them it is the only authority on earth to use the power of God. I tell them it is to heal and comfort. They all explain to me that prayer does the same thing, and that millions are healed because of prayer, so what do you need the priesthood for? Can you help me know what to explain to them? Thanks,

Sheila

Dear Sheila,

Both the prayer of faith and the power of the priesthood are effective in calling down blessings from heaven. James tells us,

> *And the prayer of faith shall save the sick, and the Lord shall raise him up; and if he have committed sins, they shall be forgiven him.* (James 5:15)

There is a difference between the efficacy of prayer and the power of the priesthood. A prayer on behalf of the sick is an appeal to the Father to intercede in their behalf. A prayer may be offered by any one of our Father's children. He will listen to and bless those who live in righteousness and who exercise faith in the Lord.

Those who hold the Holy Priesthood, however, speak officially in the name of Jesus Christ, and, through the inspiration of the Holy Spirit, may invoke the blessings of the Father on those who are ill. Brigham Young said,

> When I lay hands on the sick, I expect the healing power and influence of God to pass through me to the patient, and the disease to give way. I do not say that I heal everybody I lay hands on; but many have been healed under my administration. (*Discourses of Brigham Young*, p. 162)

The power of the priesthood goes far beyond the blessing of the sick. The priesthood is the power by which worlds are organized and brought into existence. It is the power through which God administers in the affairs of men. Through the power of the priesthood the true and living Church was restored to the earth, and therein through that same power are the ordinances of salvation administered. President John Taylor added,

> This same power has also been abundantly manifested in these latter days in the midst of the Saints of God, in deliverances from evil, in escapes from enemies, in the quelling of mobs, in the stilling of the angry waves of the sea, in the healing of the sick, in the casting out of unclean spirits, and in many other miraculous manifestations of the power and goodness of God, and of the authority with which He has invested His servants who are endowed and clothed upon with the Priesthood, which is endless and after the order of the Son of God. (*Mediation and Atonement*, Ch.10)

—Gramps

WHY IS THE BIBLE NOT MORE CONSISTENT IN DECLARING THE LINEAGE OF ABRAHAM?

Dear Gramps,

There are various references in the Bible to the lineage of Abraham—House of Israel, Family of Jacob, House of David, Israel, etc. Why is there not more consistency? It seems to me that there are distinctions, otherwise why the variety of terms? For example, the lineage of Abraham would include Esau and his descendants—am I making this clear?

P.S. Thanks for the answer to the lost 10 tribes.

Mary Jane

Dear Mary Jane,

Abraham was highly favored of the Lord and received from him a great promise, found in Abraham 2:9-11

> And I will make of thee a great nation, and I will bless thee above measure, and make thy name great among all nations, and thou shalt be a blessing unto thy seed after thee, that in their hands they shall bear this ministry and Priesthood unto all nations;
>
> And I will bless them through thy name; for as many as receive this Gospel shall be called after thy name, and shall be accounted thy seed, and shall rise up and bless thee, as their father;
>
> And I will bless them that bless thee, and curse them that curse thee; and in thee (that is, in thy Priesthood) and in thy seed (that is, thy Priesthood), for I give unto thee a promise that this right shall continue in thee, and in thy seed after thee (that is to say, the literal seed, or the seed of the body) shall all the families of the earth be blessed, even with the blessings of the Gospel, which are the blessings of salvation, even of life eternal.

Among the great blessings here promised to Abraham are three significant things to consider: 1) that the rights of the priesthood would be given to and administered through his descendants; 2) that whoever receives and obeys the gospel of Jesus Christ will be adopted into his lineage, receiving the rights of all the promised blessings; and 3) that through the administration of the priesthood by the descendants of Abraham shall all the nations of the earth be blessed.

At the death of Abraham the Lord reaffirmed this blessing on the head of his son, Isaac.

> And it came to pass after the death of Abraham, that God blessed his son Isaac; and Isaac dwelt by the well Lahairoi. (Genesis 25:11)

Isaac had two sons, Esau and Jacob. Although Esau was the older, and as such would normally receive the rights of the firstborn, nevertheless, through a deception instigated by his mother, Rebecca (Genesis 17:1-27), the father's blessing was given to Jacob instead of to Esau.

> Therefore God give thee of the dew of heaven, and the fatness of the earth, and plenty of corn and wine: Let people serve thee, and nations bow down to thee: be lord over thy brethren, and let thy mother's sons bow down to thee: cursed be every one that curseth thee, and blessed be he that blesseth thee. (Genesis 27:28-29)

Jacob's name was changed to Israel. (Genesis 32:28) He, through his four wives, had 12 sons, whose descendants have come to be known as the 12 tribes of Israel. These 12 tribes are the heirs of the blessings of Abraham and the inheritors of the rights of the Holy Priesthood, and through them all the nations of the earth are being, and will yet be, blessed.

Now, as to the terminology used in the scriptures referring to these families and their lineage, we encounter both synonyms and homonyms. The *seed* of Abraham and the *children* of Abraham, are synonymous expressions for the *descendants* of Abraham. We have the *house* of Israel and the *children* of Israel as synonymous terms. And the term *house* in this sense is also synonymous with the word *tribe*. But the word *house* is a homonym with serval meanings. Of course it refers to a dwelling, such as "the house of the Lord," referring to the temple. It also refers to a family, as those that live in a house, or to an extended family which would include the relatives of the head of the house, as in 2 Samuel 3:1:

> Now there was long war between the house of Saul and the house of David: but David waxed stronger and stronger, and the house of Saul waxed weaker and weaker.

So we have the words *descendants, family, children, house* and *tribe,* all used as synonyms relating to the covenant people of the Lord. Each of these synonymous terms is also used as homonyms in various applications in the scripture.

How are we to know which definition of each word was intended by the original author? There are a variety of interpretations of much of the scripture—witness the large number of different church denominations with their varied beliefs, who all take their different doctrines from the same Bible. To understand the intent of the scriptural authors and the meaning of the scriptures, we cannot apply to an analysis of definition, etymology, sentence structure or word usage, because all will admit to various possibilities. There is, however, a sure and unequivocal method by which the true meaning of any scriptural passage may be determined. Paul tells us *for what man knoweth the things of a man, save the spirit of man which is in him? even so the things of God knoweth no man, but the Spirit of God* (1 Corinthians 2:11), and that *the natural man receiveth not the things of the Spirit of God: for they are foolishness unto him: neither can he know them, because they are spiritually discerned.* (1 Corinthians 2:14)

Thus, the scriptures, as they treat the things of the spirit and the things of eternity, can never be understood without the aid and inspiration of the Holy Spirit. Paul, who was a learned man in his day, did not rely on the power of his own intellect to understand the scriptures, Rather, he confesses,

> *Now we have received, not the spirit of the world, but the spirit which is of God; that we might know the things that are freely given to us of God. Which things also we speak, not in the words which man's wisdom teacheth, but which the Holy Ghost teacheth; comparing spiritual things with spiritual.* (1 Corinthians 2:12-13)

Those of us who have been baptized into the Church of Jesus Christ of Latter-day Saints have had bestowed upon us in an authoritative way the Gift of the Holy Ghost. To apply this gift to the understanding of scripture we must first live a life of sufficient worthiness that we may receive the gift that has been bestowed on us. (See Mosiah 2:37; Alma 7:21; Alma 34:36; Helaman 4:24) Then it is necessary to appeal to the Lord in prayer that he will reveal to us the meaning and intent of His word. *And it is my will that you shall humble yourselves before me, and obtain this blessing by your diligence and humility and the prayer of faith.* (D&C 104:79) Then it is necessary to study, ponder, reflect, examine, compare, and do as much as is in our power to understand what we read. Associated with this activity we must listen to and be perceptive to "the still small voice"—the whisperings of the Holy Spirit—*And it came to pass when they heard this voice, and beheld that it was not a voice of thunder, neither was it a voice of a great tumultuous noise, but behold, it was a still voice of perfect mildness, as if it had been a whisper, and it did pierce even to the very soul.* (Helaman 5:30) By diligent application of these principles in the frequent reading and study of the scriptures, we will come to understand by personal revelation from the divine source itself the meaning and intent of the word of God.

—Gramps

HOW WERE MISSIONARIES TRAINED IN THE LATE 1800's?

Hi,

I'm trying to get historical information on the training/ instruction missionaries would have received in the late 1800's. My great-grandfather served a mission to New Zealand from 1889-1892 and (from his journals) had quite a time learning the Maori language and I'm curious to know what, if any, training they went through before leaving. Thanks! (And I really enjoy Mormon Town and all the work you're doing.)

Helen

Dear Helen,

I'm not sure what the missionary training was like in the late 1800's, but let me tell you what it was like in the 1940's, and it may shed some light on your question.

I went into what they called in those days the Mission Home, in June, 1946. Missionaries were held there for about a week and were instructed by the General Authorities on the various aspects of missionary work. No language training was given. In those days, mission calls were for two and half years—I suppose the extra six months were to give time for the missionaries to learn the language after arriving in the mission field.

In my case, we had to leave after only four days to take a train to New York City and there secure our visas to Argentina in time to board the Argentine freighter, Rio Santa Cruz. It took us 31 days after leaving New York to arrive in Buenos Aires.

—Gramps

WILL THE CHINESE INVADE OUR LAND IN THE LAST DAYS?

Dear Gramps,

I have really enjoyed your answers to many questions I have had over the years, and know that the question I have you will be able to answer. In a recent Sacrament meeting a visiting speaker related several statements that he attributed to Joseph Smith. He stated in one of them that in the last days that the Chinese would invade our land. I may not have remembered it word for word, but was quite startled, as I had never heard this before,

can you shed any light on this? If not I can find the Brethren and ask them. Thanking you for your wonderful answers…
Dorene

Dear Dorene,
I have looked at over 50 references that include both Joseph Smith and China, and in none of them did I find any hint of any type of invasion by China. Nor have I ever heard of such a thing. President Hinckley is reported to have said on one occasion that the church would be a lot worse off because of all the false doctrine that is preached from the pulpits, except that so few people are listening.
—Gramps

WAS THERE MORE THAN ONE QUORUM OF TWELVE APOSTLES IN THE TIME OF CHRIST

Dear Gramps,
I sometimes wonder, how come in the time of Christ were there more than one set of apostles called and why there is only THE twelve apostles today. What I mean is that Jesus called his apostles, those who ministered with him; then when he was resurrected and visited the Americas, he called another twelve apostles to minister unto the people there (unless I'm reading it wrong). Also, was there a possibility that he called others in other lands? Hope you can shed some insight as no one is quite sure.
Many thanks,
C.A. Smith

Dear C.A.
The special ministers called from among the Nephites by the Savior when He appeared to them after his resurrection were not called apostles, but rather disciples or ministers. Nephi was shown in vision the advent of the Savior among his descendants. The account of that vision speaks of *the twelve apostles of the Lamb*, who were those called to preside over the Church at Jerusalem, and who would act as judges over the twelve ministers or disciples who were called to preside over the Church in the Land of Promise.
> *And I saw the heavens open, and the Lamb of God descending out of heaven; and he came down and showed himself unto them. And I also saw and bear record that the Holy Ghost fell upon twelve others; and they were ordained of God, and chosen. And the angel spake unto me, saying:*

Behold the <u>twelve disciples</u> of the Lamb, who are chosen to minister unto thy seed. And he said unto me: Thou rememberest the <u>twelve apostles</u> of the Lamb? Behold they are they who shall judge the twelve tribes of Israel; wherefore, the <u>twelve ministers</u> of thy seed shall be judged of them; for ye are of the house of Israel. And these <u>twelve ministers</u> whom thou beholdest shall judge thy seed. And, behold, they are righteous forever; for because of their faith in the Lamb of God their garments are made white in his blood. (1 Nephi 12:6-10)*

When the Savior appeared before the Nephites after his resurrection, one of the first things He did was to call Nephi and eleven others and give them authority to baptize. (3 Nephi 12:1) In 3 Nephi 15:11-12 He cites them as his disciples, and in 3 Nephi 18:37 He gives them the power to bestow the Holy Ghost. The names of the twelve disciples are given in 3 Nephi 19:4.

These disciples administered among their people much as the twelve apostles did among the church in the Old World.

And there were great and marvelous works wrought by the disciples of Jesus, insomuch that they did heal the sick, and raise the dead, and cause the lame to walk, and the blind to receive their sight, and the deaf to hear; and all manner of miracles did they work among the children of men; and in nothing did they work miracles save it were in the name of Jesus. (4 Nephi 15)

As the church has grown in the days of the restoration, the administration of the affairs of the Kingdom has been modified to fit the circumstances. In earlier times, for instance, quarterly stake conferences were held, presided over and attended by members of the Twelve. As the Church grew, more and more authority was delegated to local officials. Today the church throughout the world is divided into administrative areas, presided over by members of the quorums of seventy, who act under the direction of the twelve apostles.

In the days of the Savior communication between the two great heads of the church was impossible, and so they acted independently of one another, but both under the active direction of the Savior. Yet, the organization was one, and the twelve disciples in land of Bountiful were and are under the authority of the twelve Apostles who served in the land of Jerusalem.

—Gramps

WHY IS THE STATUE OF MORONI
ON THE TEMPLES?

Gramps,
Why is Moroni on the top of the temples when Michael is supposed to be the arch angel. Thanks,
Shelly

Dear Shelly,
Moroni is the angel of the restoration. He appeared to Joseph Smith for the first time on September 21, 1823, in answer to the prophet's inquiring prayer. This great vision is recorded in the Pearl of Great Price. I'm sure you know the history of how the Angel Moroni appeared each year thereafter for four years, schooling the young prophet. Then he delivered to Joseph the plates upon which the Book of Mormon was anciently written, which contain the fullness of the everlasting gospel. The statue of the angel Moroni on the temples is cast in the act of sounding a trumpet. We may take this to symbolize the sounding of the gospel that is to be preached to every nations, kindred, tongue and people.
—Gramps

IS CAFFEINATED POP AGAINST
THE WORD OF WISDOM?

Hi Gramps,
Ever since joining the church five years ago, I have wondered about the issue of drinking caffeinated pop. The missionaries that taught us, said we should drink 7up, Sprite, etc…without the caffeine. Upon joining, we gave up all colas. Within a few months, I noticed many members use cola drinks frequently. When my daughter went on a youth trip and rode with the bishop she came home and told us he drank Coke all the way there and back. Shortly after that my family gradually began using colas again. I have to admit, I felt better and more spiritually in tune while abstaining from caffeine. But, I wonder, what is the church's stand on this issue? Thanks,
Sherry

Dear Sherry,

Section 89 of the Doctrine and Covenants, known as the Word of Wisdom, was received on 27 February 1833 at a meeting of the School of the Prophets in the upper room of the Whitney store in Kirtland, Ohio. It was published on a broadsheet in December 1833, and included as Section 80 in the 1835 edition of the Doctrine & Covenants.

Although the Word of Wisdom was given by the Lord to the Prophet Joseph Smith "not by commandment or constraint" but "given for a principle with promise," it is nevertheless a binding document on the members of the Church. To quote from the *Millennial Star*, 1 February 1852, p. 35,

> The Word of Wisdom became a binding document on the members of the Church at the general conference on 9 Sept. 1851. President Brigham Young proposed to the general conference that all saints formally covenant to abstain from tea, coffee, tobacco and whiskey and "all things mentioned in the Word of Wisdom." The motion was accepted unanimously and became binding as a commandment for all members thereafter.

Supporting the point that Section 89 was binding on the members of the Church, Brigham Young said on April 7, 1869,

> I know that some say the revelations upon these points are not given by way of commandment. Very well, but we are commanded to observe every word that proceeds from the mouth of God. (*Discourses of Brigham Young*, pp. 182-83)

Although the Word of Wisdom, as a formal document, is binding on the members of the Church, other harmful substances are not under the same official proscription. However, the brethren have counseled against taking into the body any harmful substances. Concerning the use of cola drinks, the following counsel is given in the Priesthood Bulletin, February 1972, p. 4.

> *Are Cola Drinks Forbidden by the Word of Wisdom?*
> What about soft drinks containing habit-forming drugs or caffeine, such as cola drinks? Although soft drinks are not mentioned specifically in the Word of Wisdom, an official statement by the Church's leaders reads: 'With reference to cola drinks, the Church has never officially taken a position on this matter, but the leaders of the Church have advised, and we do now specifically advise, against the use of any drink containing harmful habit-forming drugs under circumstances that would result in acquiring the habit. Any beverage that contains ingredients harmful to the body should be avoided.

There are some who would like to walk as close to the line of disobedience as they are allowed, and participate in the pleasures of the world to the extent that their standing in the Church would permit. It is a much safer practice to walk as far away from the line of disobedience as possible. It may be exciting, for instance, to walk along the edge of a cliff and get the thrill of looking over the edge. However, one false step—tripping over a twig or stepping on a loose stone—and one is in severe danger of falling over the cliff and being wounded on the rocks below. How much more sensible it is to take the path along the top of the ridge where any little accident would mean nothing more that brushing oneself off and continuing on the way.

One of the purposes of this life is to become the masters of ourselves, controlling what we say, do and think. If we become addicted to any habit forming drug, to that extent we are enslaved rather than being in control.

—Gramps

DOES GOD POSSESS FOREKNOWLEDGE?

Hey Gramps,

No one can answer my question to the fullest, so I hope you can. In the pre-existence we are all spirits and already know our families, earthly sisters, brothers, moms, and dads, right? Okay, next question...How could God know about fertility drugs and sextuplets being born? Meaning...how could there have been a spirit for each sextuplet if God had no clue fertility drugs would be discovered and change the way of pregnancies? I'm not sure if I worded that all right, but I hope you can answer. Thanks,

Tia

Dear Tia,

By your question you apparently assume that God knows only the present and the past, but cannot know the future because it hasn't happened yet. This is not really the case. We have the concepts of 'time' and 'eternity'. We are well acquainted with the concept of time because we live in an environment of time, and it's difficult for us to imagine anything else because it is not part of our experience. But the scriptures tell us some interesting things in this regard.

Time only is measured unto men . (Alma 40:8)

Q. What are we to understand by the book which John saw, which was sealed on the back with seven seals?

We are to understand that it contains the revealed will, mysteries, and the works of God; the hidden things of his economy concerning this earth during the seven thousand years of its continuance, or its <u>temporal existence</u> (D&C 77:6), in other words, its existence in *time*.

God is not restricted by temporal constraints because he lives in eternity, where time does not exist. In fact, at the beginning of the millennium an astounding event will occur in which six angels will appear and will reveal the secret acts of men, and the mighty works of God in each of the six thousand years since the advent of Adam. Then will another angel appear and *shall sound his trump; and he shall stand forth upon the land and upon the sea, and swear in the name of him who sitteth upon the throne, that there shall be time no longer.* (D&C 88:110)

Not only does God have all knowledge, but He sees into the future. He looks across time in the same manner that we look across space.

For if our heart condemn us, God is greater than our heart, and knoweth all things. (1 John 3:20)

God knoweth all things. (Mormon 8:17)

They [the angels] *reside in the presence of God, on a globe like a sea of glass and fire, where all things for their glory are manifest, <u>past, present, and future, and are continually before the Lord</u>*. (D&C 130:7)

If you would like a little more in-depth treatment of the concept of the limited nature of time, you might look at an article entitled, *There Shall be Time No Longer*, that can be found under "Articles by H. C. Gorton" in the web site, www.h.clay.gorton. com.

—Gramps

IS IT OK TO GROUP DATE AT AGE 14?

Hey Gramps,

I have a couple of questions. My questions concern dating. I have never heard anyone say this but I heard that you can group date when you are 14. My question is, what does group dating include? Could/ should it just be called "hanging out" or "getting together" with a group of friends? I was also wondering when we are 16 are we allowed to single date or are we supposed to double date until we are 18 and then begin single dating? And when are we advised to begin steady dating? I have one more question: Is it OK to kiss before you have turned 16? I mean by this, kissing on the hand or cheek...I was just wondering...Thanks!!!!!

CTR, Princess Dani

Dear Princess Dani,

There are approved programs where boys and girls may have joint activities at age 14. These activities vary from ward to ward and from stake to stake. It is very wise to follow the counsel of your parents, your bishop and your youth leaders. They are all extremely interested in your welfare, and will help the youth to plan activities that are wholesome, uplifting, worthwhile and fun.

We live in a very dangerous age. Immorality, one of the greatest evils in the sight of God, has become commonplace. As you undoubtedly know, much pressure is placed on young people with appropriately high moral values to participate in activities of an unsavory nature. Such activities should be avoided like the plague! You must have a CTR ring. What a wonderful constant reminder to always make proper choices! Young people are cautioned not to date, and to associate with members of the opposite sex only in approved group activities until they are at least 16 years old. However, nothing magical happens on your sixteenth birthday. You are still the same person you were the day before, when you were only 15. The transition from group to individual social activities with members of the opposite sex should be gradual, well monitored and still under the direction and supervision of your parents and bishop.

These teenage years can be the most wonderful, exciting and fun years of your life; or they can be the most difficult, frustrating and painful years. The thing that many young people fail to realize is that they are completely in the driver's seat as to which path they will take. You make the choices regarding whom you will go with, where you will go and what you will do. As has been said, we are always free to make choices, but we are never free from the consequences of those choices. And if we make unwise choices during these most important formative years, it will affect our lives forever after. We should always remember never to sacrifice what we want most for what we want now.

You ask about progressing from dating different fellows to steady dating. It seems that there are at least a couple of reasons for steady dating. One reason is to provide the security that you will always have a partner for social activities. The other reason is that you have made a commitment with someone for marriage and are awaiting the date. There are several reasons why steady dating should be avoided. One, it becomes easy when a commitment to steady date has been made, to get together for little or no reason—just to fulfill the implied commitment to be together. Such frequent association without a planned objective can easily lead into situations of increased familiarity, which also should be avoided like the plague. Another important reason is that one cuts herself off from getting to know and associate with a variety of boys. You could be missing out on meeting someone really wonderful.

Another subject that might be broached is, whom should one date? Let me tell you an obvious truism: You will marry someone with whom at one time you had a first date. When we begin dating, emotional involvements quickly follow. We may be attracted by any number of good points of someone who also has a number of unsavory or inappropriate qualities or characteristics. It is very easy to shut our eyes to the bad things because we are attracted by the good things. One of the most crucial decisions we will ever make in our lives is to decide whom we will marry. Since you are going to marry someone with whom you had a first date once, wouldn't it be wise to restrict your dating to those boys who would qualify to be worthy husbands? If I were in your position and found a boy who was interested in me and in whom I was interested that was not living a completely worthy life, I think I would tell him something like this: "Look, I think you're a really great kid, and I think it would be fun going on a date with you. And I'll be happy to do that as soon as you start coming to Church—quit smoking—clean up your language—promise to keep your hands to yourself—stop running around with that crowd—" Whatever!

Now, about kissing on a date. What does kissing mean? Why do we do it? It is one thing to kiss your father and mother goodnight, and it is quite another thing when alone with a boy to start kissing one another. That activity is often the first step to arouse the emotions, and when we are emotionally involved our judgement becomes impaired! The problem is, we think we are in control of our emotions when in reality we are not.

Let me tell you a little story about a train engineer on a freight train heading for the end of the line in, say, Boston, Massachusetts. Depending on the speed the train is going, on the weight of the train and on the friction between the wheels and the track, the engineer must put on the brakes at a certain distance from the station, or the train won't stop before it comes to the end of the track. Let's say that the engineer was distracted. He was looking at some interesting scene along the track, or his mind was on some other subject and he passed the critical point without applying the brakes. The train will crash! The engineer may still feel that he is in control; however, he can stomp on the brakes with all his might, he can wish with all his heart that he had been paying attention, he can promise himself that he will never to it again—the train will crash anyway. He has gone beyond the point of no return without realizing it.

Emotional situations are much the same way. We must know when to put on the brakes, where not to go beyond the line. And those decisions cannot be made while we are emotionally involved. They must be made when we are in full control of our faculties, in the quiet of our own home, hopefully in consultation with parents who know all about the path that you are traveling and are more desirous than many realize for your best welfare and happiness. We wish you much happiness in the exciting adventure of life!

—Gramps

WHAT HAPPENED TO CAIN?

Dear Gramps,
Is Cain still wandering the earth like a vagabond until Christ comes again—or what actually happened to him?
Marc

Dear Marc,
The birth date and the death date of Cain are not known, but there is no scriptural evidence that his life was extended beyond its natural span. The reference to being a fugitive and a vagabond is found in Moses 5:39:

> *Behold thou hast driven me out this day from the face of the Lord, and from thy face shall I be hid; and I shall be a fugitive and a vagabond in the earth; and it shall come to pass, that he that findeth me will slay me, because of mine iniquities, for these things are not hid from the Lord.*

In the phrase, *"he that findeth me will slay me,"* the pronoun, "me" refers to Cain and his descendants. In responding to Cain's lament, the Lord replied (Moses 5:40),

> *And I the Lord said unto him: Whosoever slayeth thee, vengeance shall be taken on him sevenfold. And I the Lord set a mark upon Cain, lest any finding him should kill him.*

The mark placed upon Cain was passed on to his descendants. It was preserved through the great flood by Egyptus, the wife of Ham, who was of the seed of Cain. Their son, Pharoah, was the first ruler of Egypt. (See Abraham 1:21-27)

—Gramps

WHAT IS THE SIGNIFICANCE OF
THE SWORD OF LABAN?

Dear Gramps,
*I know that the sword of Laban became significant to the Nephites as it
was mentioned a few times in the Book of Mormon. I also know that Joseph
Smith found the sword of Laban with the plates. So my question is, what is
the significance of the sword of Laban? Thanx,*
Abbie

Dear Abbie,
During Nephite times the sword of Laban apparently was a symbol of
kingly authority, as it was given, along with the sacred records, to each suc-
ceeding Nephite king. The sword of Laban was included in the various
relics that were given to Joseph Smith, along with the plates of the Book of
Mormon. The Three Witnesses to the Book of Mormon were promised a
view of the sword of Laban, along with the breastplate and the Urim and
Thummim. (D&C 10:1)

It is also recorded that Joseph Smith and Oliver Cowdery saw the sword
of Laban on two occasions when they entered a cave in the Hill Cumorah.

"The first time they went there the sword of Laban hung upon the wall;
but when they went again it had been taken down and laid upon the table
across the gold plates; it was unsheathed, and on it was written these words:
'This sword will never be sheathed again until The Kingdoms of this world
become the Kingdom of our God and his Christ'." (JD 19:38)

There is a treatise in the "Journal of Book of Mormon Studies" entitled,
"The Sword of Laban as a Symbol of Divine Authority and Kingship," The
abstract to that paper includes the statement: "The sword of Laban as it is
associated with Joseph Smith came to be an additional witness of his
authority and of the divine sanction for his work."

—Gramps

WHERE DO DOGS GO WHEN THEY DIE?

Gramps,
*I would like to know where dogs go when they die. I had a dog that
died and she was like family. I would like to know if we will be with her
in the next life. Is there a special place they go or will she be with us?
Please let me know because I'm very interested in knowing about it.*
John and Teresa

Dear John and Teresa,

In the first place, we know that all things were created spiritually before they were created temporally. In Moses 3:7 we read,

> *And I, the Lord God, formed man from the dust of the ground, and breathed into his nostrils the breath of life; and man became a living soul, the first flesh upon the earth, the first man also; <u>nevertheless, all things were before created; but spiritually were they created and made according to my word</u>.*

We also know that through the infinite atonement of the Savior all living things will be resurrected, the spirit reunited with the body, and will participate in eternal life. In *Answers to Gospel Questions,* by Joseph Fielding Smith, we read the following:

> "Question: Do animals have spirits? If so, will they obtain the resurrection, and if so, where will they go?
>
> "Answer: The simple answer is that animals do have spirits and that through the redemption made by our Savior they will come forth in the resurrection to enjoy the blessing of immortal life."

Will the animals that we knew in mortality be with us in the eternity? Again, Joseph Fielding Smith has provided a definitive answer:

> It would be a very strange world where animals were not found. If, after the resurrection of the dead, we discovered that man was the only living creature with immortality, we would certainly consider it a very strange world. (*Doctrines of Salvation,* Vol.1, p.63)
>
> So we see that the Lord intends to save not only the earth and the heavens, not only man who dwells upon the earth, but all things which he has created. The animals, the fishes of the sea, the fowls of the air, as well as man, are to be recreated, or renewed, through the resurrection, for they too are living souls." (*Doctrines of Salvation,* Vol.1, p.74)

Since we will live on the earth during the millennium and, if we are worthy, on the sanctified and celestialized earth in the eternities, we would imagine that the good things of the earth, both plants and animals, will continue to be a part of it, so that we would continue to enjoy their company and they ours.

—Gramps

AM I DOOMED TO BE BALD?

Gramps,
I liked your cat theory. My question is: My grandpa was bald, my dad is bald, my baby brother is bald. What are the chances of me going bald? And what's up with my mom, she's going bald too. Thanks...
A clueless guy in Korea

Dear Clueless,
Have you looked at your own head lately?
—Gramps

WHY WERE THE MARKS OF CHRIST'S CRUCIFIXION RETAINED AFTER HIS RESURRECTION?

Dear Gramps,
In Sunday School last week, an interesting question was raised that has left me thinking. Why is it that when Christ appeared to Mary (and others) in His resurrected state, and showed Mary the prints in His hands, that the prints were there? If Christ's body was resurrected at that point, why were there prints in His hands? I thought that when you were resurrected, that your body was in its perfect state. Is Christ's body in its perfect state with or without the prints in His hands? Your insight would be greatly appreciated.
Tom

Dear Tom,
It is true that in the resurrection everything shall be restored to its perfect frame. We read the following in Alma:
> *The spirit and the body shall be reunited again in its perfect form; both limb and joint shall be restored to its proper frame.* (Alma 11:43)

However, the Savior retained the marks of his crucifixion to be demonstrated as undeniable evidence that He is indeed the person put to death on Calvary, who suffered for the sins of all humanity and who is indeed the Savior and Redeemer of the world. He first used these marks to demonstrate to the Nephites who he was, as we read in 3 Ne. 11:14-15:
> *Arise and come forth unto me, that ye may thrust your hands into my side, and also that ye may feel the prints of the nails in my hands and in*

*my feet, that ye may know that I am the God of Israel, and the God of the
whole earth, and have been slain for the sins of the world.*

*And it came to pass that the multitude went forth, and thrust their
hands into his side, and did feel the prints of the nails in his hands and in
his feet; and this they did do, going forth one by one until they had all
gone forth, and did see with their eyes and did feel with their hands, and
did know of a surety and did bear record, that it was he, of whom it was
written by the prophets, that should come.*

The Savior will retain these marks as evidence of who He is at least to
the time of His coming in *the clouds of heaven with power and great glory,*
and will show His wounds to the unbelieving of that day, as told by
Zachariah:

*And it shall come to pass in that day, saith the LORD of hosts, that I
will cut off the names of the idols out of the land, and they shall no more
be remembered: and also I will cause the prophets and the unclean spirit
to pass out of the land....And one shall say unto him, What are these
wounds in thine hands? Then he shall answer, Those with which I was
wounded in the house of my friends.* (Zechariah 13:2-6)

—Gramps

ARE THERE MANY PATRIARCHAL BLESSINGS WHERE THE RECIPIENTS ARE FROM TRIBES OTHER THAN EPHRAIM OR MANASSEH?

Dear Gramps:

*After reading your answer about how lineage is determined in the
Church, I have a question. Everyone I know is told through patriarchal
blessings that they are of Ephraim or Manasseh. My patriarchal blessing,
however, says I am of the House of Joseph. How often to we hear of "odd"
designations like that and what do they mean?*

PLG

Dear PLG,

It is normal for patriarchs to specify the lineage of the person through
the particular tribe of the House of Israel. I am told that by far the great
majority of those receiving patriarchal blessings are declared to have come
from either the House of Ephraim or the House of Manasseh. If your patriarch has not been that specific in your case, you may want to get in touch

with him and ask if it were appropriate for him to further declare your lineage.

—Gramps

WHAT ARE THE FIVE PROCLAMATIONS OF THE CHURCH?

Dear Gramps,
What are the five proclamations that have been issued by the Church? I know the 5th proclamation had to do with the family, but where can I get information on the other four? Thanks.
Debra

Dear Debra

Here are the five official proclamations put out by the Church and a brief summary of their content.

(1) Proclamation of the First Presidency on January 15, 1841, at Nauvoo, Illinois. This document, signed by Joseph Smith, Sidney Rigdon, and Hyrum Smith, reviews the progress of the Church in spite of hardships and persecution, and speaks at length on the prospects of the settlement of Nauvoo.

(2) Proclamation of the Twelve Apostles on April 6, 1845, in New York City, and on October 22, 1845, in Liverpool, England. The Proclamation of 1845 was issued by the Twelve only, because at that time there was no First Presidency due to the martyrdom of the Prophet Joseph Smith on June 27, 1844, and a new First Presidency was not organized until December 1847. The proclamation was apparently made in response to a revelation given January 19, 1841. (D&C 124:1-11) It was first printed in a sixteen-page pamphlet in New York City on April 6, 1845, and again in Liverpool, England, October 22, 1845. It was addressed to the rulers and people of all nations. This document was an announcement that God had spoken from the heavens and had restored the gospel of Jesus Christ to the earth. It spoke of blessings and of punishments to come, issued a warning voice, and invited all who were interested to assist in the building of the kingdom of God on the earth in preparation for the Savior's second coming. On October 3, 1975, President Ezra Taft Benson, president of the Quorum of the Twelve Apostles, spoke of this proclamation and quoted portions of it in his general conference address. (*Ensign* 15 Oct. 1975: 32-34)

(3) Proclamation of the First Presidency and the Twelve Apostles on October 21, 1865, in Salt Lake City, Utah. This document was issued to members of the Church to correct certain theories about the nature of God that had been published by one of the Twelve in official Church literature, without having those statements cleared and verified by the First Presidency and the Twelve.

(4) Proclamation from the First Presidency and the Quorum of the Twelve Apostles, April 6, 1980, issued from Fayette, New York. This document was put forth in commemoration of the 150th anniversary of the organization of the Church. On Sunday, April 6, 1980, a portion of the Sunday morning session of General Conference was broadcast from the newly reconstructed Peter Whitmer, Sr., home in Fayette, New York. President Spencer W. Kimball spoke briefly of the organization of the Church that had occurred on that very spot of ground. He then announced that the Church had a proclamation to declare. President Kimball's concluding words were: "Now, my brothers and sisters, with the future before us, and sensing deeply the responsibilities and divine mission of the restored Church on this sacred occasion, the First Presidency and the Quorum of the Twelve Apostles declare to the world a proclamation. We have felt it appropriate to issue this statement from here, where the Church began. Accordingly, I shall ask Elder Gordon B. Hinckley of the Quorum of the Twelve Apostles, to speak in my behalf and in behalf of my brethren, to read this proclamation to you and to the world." (CR, Apr. 1980, p. 74)

(5) A Proclamation to the World, The First Presidency and Council of the Twelve Apostles of the Church of Jesus Christ of Latter-day Saints, September 23, 1995. This document extols the sanctity of the family and the marriage covenant, and warns against immoral behavior.

—Gramps

SHOULD LDS PEOPLE BE INVOLVED IN HYPNOSIS?

Dear Gramps,

I am wondering what your and the church's opinion is on hypnosis for regaining memory from childhood? Is hypnosis ever a thing for LDS to be involved in? Another question: Why would a loving God allow such atrocities as child abuse to occur? I understand the concept of free agency, but how can God not interfere with a person's free agency when an innocent child (who has no free agency) is being abused? I just don't understand. Thanks.

Name withheld,

Dear Withheld,

Hypnosis is often used in the entertainment world, frequently to invoke embarrassing situations that are supposed to be perceived as humorous. I would recommend staying completely away from all such demonstrations. However, in the hands of trained and responsible professionals hypnotism can be a valuable tool in restoring memory, influencing the involuntary response system, and in treating certain ailments. In a letter addressed to Dr. Leslie Cooper on 7 October 1974, Church Commissioner of Health Dr. James O. Mason, noted that the First Presidency had cleared the following statement on hypnosis:

> The Church regards the use of hypnosis under competent, professional supervision for the treatment of disease as wholly a medical question. The Church advises members against participation in hypnosis demonstrations.

With respect to your second question, it is important to try to understand the inequities of human behavior from the broader spectrum of eternity. Our minds are closed to our pre-mortal existence, but it is entirely possible that we were not ignorant of what would or could happen in mortality before we entered on the mortal stage.

Apart from that, the greatest gift that God has given to man is his free agency. God will not use coercion to rectify human ills until humanity becomes so steeped in iniquity that there is no chance for repentance. However, anyone who perpetrates iniquity, if he does not fully and thoroughly repent, will pay the full price to an eternal justice for all his wickedness. Those who have been mistreated will no doubt be recompensed by the Lord for whatever suffering they have undergone that is not of their own doing. We must remember that the Lord will leave no one in His debt. His loving kindness and compassion have infinite dimensions, and he will bandage up the broken hearted, and wipe away the tear from every eye. Justice will not be denied.

In addition it must be remembered that this life is a testing and proving ground. The scheme of mortality is to overcome evil. Evil must be present in order for us to gain faith in the Lord, Jesus Christ, gain strength of character, and demonstrate to the Lord that we will be obedient especially in the face of trial, difficulty and opposition. The Lord has counseled,

Therefore, he giveth this promise unto you, with an immutable covenant that they shall be fulfilled; and all things wherewith you have been afflicted shall work together for your good, and to my name's glory, saith the Lord. (D&C 98:3)

Therefore, be not afraid of your enemies, for I have decreed in my heart, saith the Lord, that I will prove you in all things, whether you will abide in my covenant, even unto death, that you may be found worthy. For if ye will not abide in my covenant ye are not worthy of me. (D&C 98: 14-15)

—Gramps

ARE SOME ORDINANCES PERFORMED IN THE NAMES OF ALL THREE MEMBERS OF THE GODHEAD?

Dear Gramps—
I've wondered for a time why is it that when we baptize we do it in the name of the Father, Son and Holy Ghost, as is also the case in the temple marriage. Why then are the other ordinances, such as confirmation, priesthood ordination, sacrament, initiatory, etc., performed only in the name of the Son?
Lisle

Dear Lisle,
The authority to act officially in the name of deity is a sacred privilege that has not existed on the earth since shortly after the Savior's mortal sojourn until the restoration of the gospel by the prophet Joseph Smith. Baptism was administered in the days of the Savior by invoking the sanction of the Father, and the Son, and the Holy Ghost. The Savior commissioned his disciples to
Go ye therefore, and teach all nations, baptizing them in the name of the Father, and of the Son, and of the Holy Ghost. (Matthew 28:19)

Think of the significance of the ordinance by which an individual may qualify to enter the Kingdom of God though the waters of baptism, and the other great ordinance by which individuals may enter into exaltation in the celestial kingdom through observing the eternal marriage covenant. These two ordinances that permit entrance into the Kingdom and into exaltation within the Kingdom are administered in the names of all three members of the Godhead. The other ordinances are for different positions and

responsibilities within the Kingdom, and are appropriately administered in the name of the Head of the Church and organization that bears His name.
   —Gramps

IS PSYCHIC COMMUNICATION WITH THE SPIRIT WORLD REAL?

Dear Gramps:
My wife, older children and I had a discussion about mystics, channelers and psychics. There was a talk show on yesterday that showcased some people who could supposedly communicate with the other side. My wife and children believed that there are truly people with these abilities. I told them the Lord does not work this way—these people have no authority to act in this capacity. It seems especially wrong to profit financially from such activities. Could you shed some light on this topic?
Paul

Dear Paul,

The world is full of charlatans who feed on the gullibility of the innocent. There is no doubt that many who profess to communicate with the spirit world fall into this category. As you may know, Houdini spent much of his life exposing such frauds. He even made a pact that if it were possible he would communicate with certain persons from the spirit world after his death. Those who waited for his communication from across the grave never reported any evidence of any post mortal word from Houdini. In addition, there was not a seance that he attended that he was not able to discover the deception that was being perpetrated.

Although there are many who falsify this communication there is also no doubt that certain individuals do communicate with departed spirits. Perhaps the prime example is found in 1 Samuel 28. Saul had banished all witches from the land, and the prophet, Samuel, had died. When the Philistines invaded his land he asked the Lord what he should do, but the heavens were silent. So Saul sought out the witch of Endor, and disguising himself, asked her to conjure up Samuel the prophet. Samuel appeared and Saul inquired what he should do. Samuel responded, "Wherefore then dost thou ask of me, seeing the Lord is departed from thee, and is become thine enemy?" Samuel then informed him that because of his wickedness the lives of both himself and his sons would be taken on the next day.

What you say is true, that the Lord does not work in this way. Communication with the spirit world is not at the demand of mortals, but rather according to the will of God. Such unauthorized communications have always been denounced by the Lord and by his servants. Perhaps the earliest injunction against such practices is found in Deuteronomy 18:10:

> *There shall not be found among you any one that maketh his son or his daughter to pass through the fire, or that useth divination, or an observer of times, or an enchanter, or a witch, or a charmer, or a consulter with familiar spirits, or a wizard, or a necromancer.*

(Necromancy is defined as the conjuration of the spirits of the dead for purposes of magically revealing the future or influencing the course of events.)

—Gramps

WHY DO I HAVE TROUBLE FEELING THE SPIRIT IN THE TEMPLE?

Dear Gramps,

I don't know if you will print my letter or not. I have not discussed this with anyone, but I do not feel about the temple like everyone I know. I have been to get my endowments, etc., but I do not feel "the spirit" there and find the ceremonies strange and confusing. I am not married to a member and sometimes feel that maybe I am subconsciously not feeling anything because I cannot have the "eternal marriage," celestial marriage, etc. I don't have any desire to go to the temple and sit in church listening to all the "year of the temple" talks, and how the members felt when they went. Am I the only one who feels like this?

BC

Dear BC,

I doubt very much that you are alone in your feelings, but let's try to address your concerns one at a time. The temple ceremonies may indeed seem strange when compared with what we know and experience in the outside world. But each part of each ceremony has a specific meaning and significance. The eternal realities that God reveals to His children in the holy temples must be represented in some manner. The important thing is not in the manner of representation, but in what the representation stands for. We live in a world of symbols. The symbols of one society or culture would indeed seem strange to those of another. Let's look at just a couple of examples.

In some of the early Polynesian cultures, when a couple were married they made a cut in the wrist of one arm of each partner, then tied the arms together so that the blood would mix and that they would then be "of one blood." That act would seem strange to us, but it symbolized a sacred concept to those who practiced it.

Let's say that you took out an insurance policy. You would sign your name at the bottom of the form indicating your agreement to pay the premiums. The form, printed by the insurance company, would state the conditions under which you would be indemnified. Your name at the bottom of the form is a symbol. It means much more than an identity of who you are. It represents in a legally binding way your commitment to honor your promise to pay. If you default on your premiums and break your promise to pay, the insurance company is under no obligation to indemnify you for any condition stated in the policy. In fact, when you do not comply with your part, the policy becomes null and void. However, if you do comply, the insurance company is legally bound to indemnify you according to the terms of the policy.

So it is with the symbols and the covenants that they represent in the temple. We should look beyond the symbols to the eternal verities that they represent. The truths revealed in the temple were given by revelation, and they can best be understood by the spirit of revelation. As we prayerfully seek to understand the significance of the endowment, the Lord will reveal to us "precept upon precept, here a line and there a line," the deep meanings of the eternal truths that are available there for us to learn.

Please do not give up hope of having an eternal marriage. If you humbly and sincerely live according to the principles that you have espoused, every promise made to you in the temple will be fulfilled. How much more can we trust in the word of the Lord than in the promises of even the most reliable insurance company! In our family my father was not a member of the Church. He was a good, honorable man whom I and my sisters and our mother loved dearly, but he would have nothing to do with the Church—until he was sixty-four years old. One day, out of the blue, he asked if he could be baptized. What a thrill it was to see my father become a member of the Church after all those years! He passed away just a few months later.

I can't promise you that every person will react to the prayers of others as did my father, but I know this; if we do our part in living righteously the

Lord will surely bless us in the way that will be for our best good. We read in D&C 98:3,

> *Therefore, he giveth this promise unto you, with an immutable covenant that they shall be fulfilled; and all things wherewith you have been afflicted shall work together for your good, and to my names' glory, saith the Lord.*

—Gramps

WHAT DOES "WHEAT FOR MAN" IN THE WORD OF WISDOM IMPLY?

Dear Gramps,

Thank you for the enlightenment you offered on the Word of Wisdom. Speaking of the Word of Wisdom, I have another question for you. In verse 17, where it says, "Nevertheless, wheat for man, and corn for the ox, and oats for the horse, and rye for the fowls and for swine and for all beasts of the field, and barley for all useful animals, and for mild drinks, as also other grain." What exactly does this mean? It seems to me that we're told that wheat to eat and barley for mild drinks are best for us "...all grains are good for the food of man...nevertheless (except) wheat for man, and corn for the ox..." etc. Are these other grains mentioned not good for us? Also rice and millet are just a few grains that aren't mentioned at all, and it seems to me that these would be part of "all grains" that are good for man because we don't see an "exception" made for them. Am I way off? I've always wanted to know what was meant by all of this. Thanks, Gramps.

Katie

Dear Katie,

I'm as curious as you are! Nevertheless, I would not suggest that the "other grains that are mentioned are not good for us," because in verse 14 we are told that "all grain is ordained for the use of man and of beasts," and in verse 16 that "all grain is good for the food of man."

Brigham Young, in 1863, told the people,

> Sixteen years ago, when we were camped upon this temple block, I told the people that there existed, in the elements around us in these mountain regions, wheat, corn, rye, oats, barley, flax, hemp, silk and every element for producing the necessary articles used by man for food, raiment and shelter. (*Journal of Discourses*, Vol.10, p.201)

Certainly some grains must be nutritionally more suited to man and others to animals. I do know that the revelation came from the Lord and that He is not capricious. The Lord has his reasons for the preference, but He indicates than none of the grains should be excluded from the diets of either man or animals.

—Gramps

WAS THE DARK SKIN OF THE CANAANITES AND THE LAMANITES ONLY FIGURATIVE?

Dear Gramps,

I would like to know if Cain and Laman and Lemuel's skin actually turned dark or if it is figurative? There is a lot of controversy about this subject. I have read these passages regularly and feel that it did indeed turn dark. Thanks,

Amy

Dear Amy,

I think that your feelings are correct. President Joseph Fielding Smith has indicated that both the Lamanites and the descendants of Cain had dark skins. We must be careful, however, not to confuse the dark skin with the curse itself. President Smith says with respect to the Lamanites that the dark skin was the <u>sign</u> of the curse. In other words, it was used as an identifier of those from whom the Spirit of the Lord had withdrawn.

> The dark skin was placed upon the Lamanites so that they could be distinguished from the Nephites and to keep the two peoples from mixing. The dark skin was the sign of the curse. The curse was the withdrawal of the Spirit of the Lord. (Joseph Fielding Smith, *Answers to Gospel Questions,* Vol. 3, p 122)

In the case of the descendants of Cain, the dark skin was actually a blessing to identify them so that they would not be slain.

> *And the LORD said unto him, Therefore whosoever slayeth Cain, vengeance shall be taken on him sevenfold. And the LORD set a mark upon Cain, lest any finding him should kill him.* (Genesis 4:15)

The curse on the descendants of Cain was that they were not permitted to hold the priesthood. President Joseph Fielding Smith identifies the mark as a black skin. See the following references:

The Cainanites, who lived in the land of Cainan, from whence Enoch came, were a righteous people and evidently were descendants of Seth. Then there must have been another people called Canaanites who were a black race and the descendants of Cain. (Joseph Fielding Smith Jr., *The Way to Perfection*, p 107)

Now the first government of Egypt was established by Pharaoh, the eldest son of Egyptus, the daughter of Ham, and it was after the manner of the government of Ham, which was patriarchal.

Pharaoh, being a righteous man, established his kingdom and judged his people wisely and justly all his days, seeking earnestly to imitate that order established by the fathers in the first generations, in the days of the first patriarchal reign, even in the reign of Adam, and also of Noah, his father, who blessed him with the blessings of the earth, and with the blessings of wisdom, but cursed him as pertaining to the Priesthood. (Abraham 1:25-26)

—Gramps

WHAT IS THE SPIRITUAL CONDITION
OF THE COMATOSE?

Hi Gramps,

I have an uncle that is living in a nursing home in somewhat of a "world of his own." There really is no communication, he cannot tell us he's hungry, hurting or anything. We just have to learn to read his body language. We used to get a smile, now not even that. I do believe he is at peace, at least I hope he is. Where is his spirit? What happens to his progression? He had had a near death experience several years ago, and describes looking down at his body. Is it possible that may be occurring now? Thanks Gramps, I await your explanation.

Janeen

Dear Janeen,

You ask some very fundamental questions, for which I am afraid there are no simple answers. Your questions relate to the subjects of free agency, responsibility, cause and effect and the judgments of God. A related question was asked the Savior by his disciples, saying,

Master, who did sin, this man, or his parents, that he was born blind? Jesus answered, Neither hath this man sinned, nor his parents: but that the works of God should be made manifest in him. (John 9:2-3)

We sometimes perceive that the wicked seem to prosper while the righteous suffer, and we wonder about the justice of God. Those thoughts presuppose that God's justice is meted out immediately, that promised rewards for righteous living and punishment for iniquity immediately follow the action. Such, of course, is not the case. Mortality is a testing ground to see *if they will do all things whatsoever the Lord their God shall command them.* (Abraham 3:25) Suffering to one degree or another is part of the test. We are commanded to

> *Search diligently, pray always, and be believing, and all things shall work together for your good, if ye walk uprightly and remember the covenant wherewith ye have covenanted one with another.* (D&C 99:24)

Not only some things will work together for our good, but "all things".

So there is a purpose in suffering. And so much of it comes near the end of life, until the body becomes an inhospitable residence for the spirit, and it must leave. There may be temporary out-of-body experiences, but one may be sure that a person's spirit belongs to his or her body until, through the process called death, the spirit departs to the spirit world, and the body, without that guiding, unifying intelligence, ceases to be a living entity and begins its decay.

Our task and objective is to maintain integrity of thought, word and action, as long as we are in possession of our faculties, so that it may be said of us,

> *Well done, thou good and faithful servant: thou hast been faithful over a few things, I will make thee ruler over many things: enter thou into the joy of thy lord.* (Matt. 25:21)

But what about when we are no longer in possession of our faculties, and become burdens on those who are responsible for us? Such circumstances provide opportunities for blessings to those who extend themselves to comfort, sooth and succor those in need. The Lord has commanded,

> *Wherefore, be faithful; stand in the office which I have appointed unto you; succor the weak, lift up the hands which hang down, and strengthen the feeble knees.* (D&C 81:5)

Showing compassion and love to those in need, and especially to those incapable of response, is a hallmark of godliness.

—Gramps

WHAT WOULD HAPPEN IF WE WERE TO TRAVEL AT THE SPEED OF LIGHT?

Dear Gramps:

Having driven with you on numerous occasions, I was wondering if you are traveling at the speed of light and you turn your headlights on, does anything happen?

Thanks,

IMYY4U2

Dear IMYY4U2,

Traveling at the speed of light with respect to what? Einstein's theory of relativity requires that time, space and mass be defined with respect to the observer's frame of reference. Thus, if you are driving your car at the speed of light, it must be with respect to some point on the road. You, however, are at rest (at least, not moving) with respect to your car. Thus, if you turned on the lights they would shine ahead at the speed of light, measured from your position in the car, whether the car was in the garage or moving away from the garage at the speed of light.

Of course, the theory of relativity does have its problems. Let's call your car a spaceship, and have two identical spaceships move away from a central point, say, the moon, in opposite directions at nine tenths the speed of light. One would suspect that the velocity of one space ship with respect to the other would be 1.8 times the speed of light. WRONG!

According to the theory of relativity, no signal can be propagated at a speed faster than the speed of light. As objects near the speed of light, the energy applied to accelerate the rate of motion is converted into the mass of the object, according to the famous equation E equals M times C squared, where E is the energy, M the mass of the object being measured and C is the velocity of light. So, if from the frame of reference of spaceship A, we measure the velocity of spaceship B, we will find that it is receding from us at a speed less than the speed of light. However, if we could measure its mass, we would find it to be heavier than our spaceship, A. Also, it would be shorter (distance is contracted in the direction of motion), and the clocks on spaceship B would be running slower than those on spaceship A. (Time slows down as we approach the speed of light.) In the limit, as the speed of light is reached, that space ship, B, would be infinitely heavy, completely flat in the direction of motion, and the clocks would all have stopped!

Now, if you can swallow all that, think about the occupants of spaceship B. They are measuring your spaceship, and find that your spaceship, A, is receding from them at near the speed of light, and that spaceship A is heavier, shorter and in it the clocks are running slower than in their spaceship, B.

Now each of those conditions is true only in relation to the frame of reference of the observer. And they are contradictory in reference to each other. It's obvious that the theory of relativity does not describe the properties of nature, but is only a practical mathematical procedure for predicting observed phenomena.

The theory of relativity in many applications is more accurate than Newton's laws of mechanics. However, as sure as the setting sun, the theory of relativity will be relegated to the dust bin of history in the same manner that has seen the demise of all the theories that have preceded it.

The Bible was compiled between the years of approx. 1400 and 400 B.C., and the Book of Mormon between the years of 600 B.C. and 400 A.D. Yet those books are as true today as the day they were written, whereas any scientific text book that you can find that is 50 years old is of no value because the concepts found therein have been proven incorrect or inadequate by subsequent scientific advance.

It reminds me of the story of the entomologist that trained an ant to obey a voice command. When the entomologist would say "Jump', the ant would jump. So the entomologist picked off the two front legs of the ant and said "Jump" and the ant still jumped. Then the entomologist picked off the middle two legs of the ant and said "Jump" and again the ant jumped. Finally, he picked off the remaining two legs of the ant and said "Jump" and the ant didn't jump. So in his final report on the project he concluded that when you remove all six legs from an ant it becomes deaf!
—Gramps

WHEN DOES THE SPIRIT ENTER THE BODY?

Dear Gramps,
Tonight the family read 3 Nephi chapter 1 about the Lord speaking to Nephi and answering his prayer saying by that he would be born the next day. What about the spirit in the womb? How could Jesus speak to Nephi and be in the womb, or does the spirit enter at birth? What's up with that, Gramps? Thanks.
Jeff

Dear Jeff,

The exact time that the pre-mortal spirit enters the mortal body is not specified in divine revelation. (See *Encyclopedia of Mormonism*, Vol.1, BIRTH) Since it is not recorded, it may not be at the same time for every person. However, there is no doubt that the Savior appeared to the Nephites as a pre-mortal spirit on the day before his birth in Bethlehem. Thus, the life of the babe in Mary's womb was sustained during that time by the life of the mother. Whether the spirit of the Savior was resident in the womb prior to his advent to the Nephites is not recorded.

Although the spirit may enter the body at some indeterminate time prior to birth, there is a time prior to that when the fetus sustains life as part of the mother. At some given time, the spirit enters the body giving it independent life. It would then be considered a mortal soul. Elder Bruce R. McConkie has touched on this subject in some of his writings. In *Doctrinal New Testament Commentary*, Vol.1, p.84, he writes

> Luke 1:41. The babe leaped in her womb In this miraculous event the pattern is seen which a spirit follows in passing from his pre-existent first estate into mortality. The spirit enters the body at the time of quickening, months prior to the actual normal birth. The value and comfort attending a knowledge of this eternal truth is seen in connection with stillborn children. Since the spirit entered the body before birth, stillborn children will be resurrected and righteous parents shall enjoy their association in immortal glory. (*Mormon Doctrine*, pp. 693-694)

There are many unanswerable questions related to the details of the spirit world and its interface with mortality. As we try to fill in the gaps between the revealed word and our observations, we must be careful to draw no conclusions that would contradict any revealed knowledge. Sometimes there is just not enough information available to answer all the questions that could come into our minds. But when we cross to the other side of the veil, where we will be able to perceive both the spirit world and mortality, I imagine that many things that are now mysterious will become obvious.

—Gramps

WHERE DID THE HOLY GHOST COME FROM?
WHAT IS THE NEW AND EVERLASTING COVENANT?

Dear Gramps,

My missionary son wrote and asked me these two questions, which I haven't been able to even begin to answer for him. I'd appreciate your help.

1. Where did the Holy Ghost come from? We know the basic origin of God and Jesus Christ, but nothing as far as I know on the origin of the third member of the Godhead.

2. Why is eternal marriage called "the NEW and everlasting covenant"? Adam and Eve were eternally sealed, so how is it new? Thanks, Jerry

Dear Jerry,

We know only that the Holy Ghost is a personage of spirit and is a member of the Godhead. Undoubtedly he was born as a spirit in the premortal existence in the same manner as all other spirits. Our Lord and Master, Jesus Christ, was the first born Son of God in the spirit world. So we must assume that the Holy Spirit is another of our Father's children, having achieved, as did the Savior, the status of Godhood while yet in the spirit world.

The meaning of the New and Everlasting Covenant was well explained by President Joseph Fielding Smith, as follows:

Each ordinance and requirement given to man for the purpose of bringing to pass his salvation and exaltation is a covenant. Baptism for the remission of sins is a covenant. When this ordinance was revealed in this dispensation, the Lord called it "a new and an everlasting covenant, even that which was from the beginning."

This covenant was given in the beginning and was lost to men through apostasy, therefore, when it was revealed again, it became to man a new covenant, although it was from the beginning, and it is everlasting since its effects upon the individual endure forever. Then again, whenever there is need for repentance, baptism is the method, or law, given of the Lord by which the remission of sins shall come, and so this law is everlasting. (Joseph Fielding Smith Jr., *Doctrines of Salvation*, Vol.1, p. 152)

—Gramps

WHAT IS THE APPROPRIATE SIZE OF FAMILIES?

Dear Gramps,

Is there anything in the scriptures or in church doctrine that tells us that we should have numerous children? So many of the people we know think they should have 8 to 11 children, but when Paul H. Dunn came to Northern California one time, he stated that it is between the wife, husband and the Lord, that the church doesn't tell us anything about this. Recently I have been asked this by several members and I don't know the answer. Please help. Thank you.

Gertrude Ruby

Dear Gertrude,

I'm sure that you will find nothing in the scriptures that would give a doctrinal basis for having large families. Although bearing and rearing children is a sacred responsibility consistent with the commandment to multiply and replenish the earth, the specific number of children that a given couple should have is left strictly up to that couple. Each couple has the right to inspiration and revelation from the Lord, if they live worthily, to give them guidance in such matters. So many factors are involved in the number of children any couple might desire to have that it would be very difficult to give even general guidelines, and there is no doubt that the number would vary depending on health, economic conditions, environmental conditions and personal preferences.

The *Encyclopedia of Mormonism* gives the following opinion on the subject:

> Decisions regarding the number and spacing of children are to be made by husband and wife together, in righteousness, and through empathetic communication, and with prayer for the Lord's inspiration. Latter-day Saints believe that persons are accountable not only for what they do but for why they do it. Thus, regarding family size and attendant questions, members should desire to multiply and replenish the earth as the Lord has commanded. In that process, God intends that his children use the agency that he has given them in charting a wise course for themselves and their families. (*The Encyclopedia of Mormonism*, Vol.1, BIRTH CONTROL)

—Gramps

How Did Joseph Smith Use
The Urim And Thummim?

Dear Gramps,

As a member of the church I have always been confronted with arguments against it. I've never really paid any attention to them but recently I heard that Joseph Smith himself used to place a special hat on his head, containing a shiny stone in order to receive a revelation!? This was described in the diaries of many people who were close to him. When I even tried to talk about this to my local church leaders, this was regarded as anti-Mormon propaganda which shouldn't be seen by members at all and I even received a warning not to bring the subject up again. This attitude almost looks like the church may be hiding something, or at least that's what I think of it...

This fact keeps bugging me, so I'm asking your opinion.

A FAIR-LDS member

Dear FAIR-LDS,

It's interesting how partial information can lead to bizarre conclusions. Sounds pretty weird, looking at a "shiny stone" in a hat. The "shiny stone" that you refer to was either the Urim and Thummin or the seer stone that Joseph was given as instruments to affect the translation of the Book of Mormon. It is well to remember that in 1829 Egyptian was a completely obscure language. The use of the hat was the most natural of occurrences. Have you ever tried to look at the numbers on a watch with a luminous dial? In order to see the luminescence the watch must be in almost complete darkness. Joseph Smith simply used a hat to exclude extraneous light so he could see what appeared on the stones into which he was looking. He didn't put it on his head. You may find this information in the following two references:

> Moreover, witnesses of the translation process consistently claim that Joseph Smith translated by placing either the Urim and Thummim or the seer stone in a hat (to obscure the light in the room) and that he did not actually translate from the physical plates. In answer to a direct question about the use of other materials, Emma Smith specifically avowed that Joseph never had any manuscripts or books to assist him in the translation. All the witnesses, directly or indirectly, provide strong evidence that Joseph Smith did not use a King James Bible. (Royal Skousen, *Review of Books on the Book of Mormon*, p. 130)

The following is David Whitmer's own statement to a reporter of the *Kansas City Journal*, published June 5, 1881...

The next day after I got there they packed up the plates and we proceeded on our journey to my father's house, where we arrived in due time, and the day after we commenced upon the translation of the remainder of the plates. I, as well as all of my father's family, Smith's wife, Oliver Cowdery and Martin Harris, were present during the translation. The translation was by Smith, and the manner as follows: He had two small stones of a chocolate color, nearly egg shape, and perfectly smooth, but not transparent, called interpreters, which were given him with the plates. He did not use the plates in the translation, but would hold the interpreters to his eyes and cover his face with a hat, excluding all light, and before his eyes would appear what seemed to be parchment, on which would appear the characters of the plates in a line at the top, and immediately below would appear the translation, in English, which Smith would read to his scribe, who wrote it down exactly as it fell from his lips. The scribe would then read the sentence written, and if any mistake had been made, the characters would remain visible to Smith until corrected, when they faded from sight to be replaced by another line. The translation at my father's occupied about one month, that is from June 1 to July 1, 1829. (See *Millennial Star*, Vol. 43, p. 421; see also *LDS Biographical Encyclopedia*, Andrew Jenson, Vol. 1, p. 263)

—*Gramps*

HOW OLD WAS ENOCH?

Dear Gramps,

Can you please tell me how old Enoch was? Genesis 5:23 says one age and Moses 8:1 says something else. Thank you.

MJM

Dear MJM,

There may be a clue to this apparent anomaly in Moses 7:68, which says, "And <u>all the days of Zion</u>, in the days of Enoch, were three hundred and sixty-five years." If we accept both Moses 7:68 and 8:1, which says, "And <u>all the days of Enoch</u> were four hundred and thirty years." then Enoch would have been 65 years old when Zion was established.

Several things happened to Enoch when he was sixty five years old. That was his age when his son, Methuselah, was born (Gen. 5:21) He was also blessed by Adam at age sixty five.

Enoch was twenty-five years old when he was ordained under the hand of Adam; and he was sixty-five and Adam blessed him. (D&C 107:48)

We read in the Joseph Smith translation of Gen. 6:26 that when he was sixty five "the Spirit of God descended out of heaven, and abode upon him."

If it were true that Zion was established when the Spirit of God descended out of heaven, and abode upon Enoch when he was sixty five, then the biblical account could be in error in referring to the age of Enoch rather than to the age of Zion when it was taken up. If this adjustment were made, than all the scriptural accounts would coincide.

—Gramps

IS GREEN TEA AGAINST THE WORD OF WISDOM?

Gramps,
What is the Church's stand on green tea. I've read that it has many healing properties. I've asked several leaders but no one knows for sure?
Thanks.
Deb

Dear Deb,
The Church's stand on green tea is that it is against the Word of Wisdom and therefore should be avoided. There is no doubt that tea and coffee contain substances that could be used for healing purposes. For instance, tea contains the three major antioxidant vitamins, C, E, and A. It also contains about 2% caffeine. Regardless of its ingredients, it has been proscribed by the Lord. The Lord specifically stated that "hot drinks are not for the body or belly." He did not elaborate on why they are not good, but He did say that those who obey the Word of Wisdom

shall receive health in their navel and marrow to their bones; and shall find wisdom and great treasure of knowledge, even hidden treasures; and shall run and not be weary, and shall walk and not faint. And...the destroying angel shall pass by them, as the children of Israel, and not slay them. (D&C 89:18-21)

Some people quibble over the wording of the Word of Wisdom because tea and coffee, per se, are not mentioned, rather the term "hot drinks" is used. Brigham Young had this to say on that subject:

Many try to excuse themselves because tea and coffee are not mentioned, arguing that it refers to hot drinks only. What did we drink hot when that Word of Wisdom was given? Tea and coffee. It definitely refers to that which we drink with our food. I said to the Saints at our last annual Conference, the Spirit whispers to me to call upon the Latter-day Saints to observe the Word of Wisdom, to let tea, coffee, and tobacco alone, and to abstain from drinking spirituous drinks. This is what the Spirit signifies through me. If the Spirit of God whispers this to His people through their leader, and they will not listen nor obey, what will be the consequence of their disobedience? Darkness and blindness of mind with regard to the things of God will be their lot; they will cease to have the spirit of prayer, and the spirit of the world will increase in them in proportion to their disobedience until they apostatize entirely from God and His ways. (*Journal of Discourses*, Vol.12, p.117, 1867)

Let us not try to rationalize disobeying the commandments because of some supposed scientific benefit, but rather exercise faith in the Lord to keep his commandments, even when, and more important, especially when that obedience requires some sacrifice on our part. Let us remember that *the wisdom of this world is foolishness with God.* (1 Cor. 3:19)
—Gramps

WHY IS ROOT BEER SO FOAMY?

Dear Gramps,
Why does root beer have so much foam in it? Other carbonated drinks don't foam that much, and I was just wondering why? So, can you answer that for me? Thanks!
Jason

Dear Jason,
In the old days when root beer was ROOT BEER, there was some intrinsic quality of the brew that gave it a rich foam. Actually, that was why it was called root beer rather than root ale or root cider, neither of which are as foamy (I am told) as beer. However, in the days of real root beer there was still a variation in the degrees of foaminess. A BOWEY'S root beer sign from the 1930's promoted its product as being "solid" or "creamy", as opposed to foamy or frothy.

However, the key to the early root beer flavor, sassafras root bark, was banned by the FDA in 1960, as it was found that a chemical compound called safrole, the principal component of sassafras, was a weak hepatic carcinogen, which causes cancer of the liver. Thus, since then root beer has been artificially flavored, just like all the other soft drinks, and the manufacturers can make it with any degree of foaminess that they want to.

But back to the original question, regardless of its history, why is root beer so foamy? Since the manufacturers won't tell us and since we have no ready means of experimentation, we will have to do as the early Greeks did. The Greek scientists, who developed much of the base of our modern reasoning process, were above experimentation. Such menial tasks were left to the slaves. They used pure logic.

The ancient Greeks were very good reasoners, but not always correct. For instance, they deduced that men had more teeth than women since men's heads were generally larger. To actually count the teeth was beneath them. So let's do a little reasoning.

The first element of foaminess is carbonation. No CO_2, no foam. Therefore, the more CO_2, the more foam. However, increasing the CO_2 content would also make the drink more pungent. (Some people would say that it would have more of a 'bite'.) So, undoubtedly, since root beer is not generally more pungent than many other soft drinks, the carbon dioxide content alone would probably not account for the foaminess.

Another factor that would be involved would be the viscosity of the liquid. As the viscosity of the soft drink is increased, the bubbles constituting the foam would have more of a tendency to form and to remain. (One doesn't get much foam on a glass of carbonated water.)

A third condition would be the surface tension of the liquid. As surface tension is increased the bubbles would have greater strength and a tendency to remain longer. So, the manufacturers of today's root beer undoubtedly play with the degree of carbonation, viscosity and surface tension in their artificially flavored concoction to produce just the degree of foaminess that they want to market. The only unfortunate aspect of the whole thing is that the artificial flavors for root beer have never been a match for the real thing.

   —Gramps

IS OUR EARTH THE MOST WICKED OF ALL THE WORLDS?

Dear Gramps,
   I have heard that our earth is the most wicked of all worlds created. If this is true, are there scriptures confirming this? Thank You
   Wm. E & Norma J.

Dear Wm. E & Norma J.

As we think about how wicked this world may be, it is well to consider how many worlds there are. Enoch said to the Lord on one occasion,

> *And were it possible that man could number the particles of the earth, yea, millions of earths like this, it would not be a beginning to the number of thy creations; and thy curtains are stretched out still; and yet thou art there.* (Moses 7:30)

Of how many particles is this earth composed? A grain of salt is about the same size as a grain of fine sand. In a teaspoon of salt there are about 8000 particles. There are three teaspoons to a tablespoon; 16 tablespoons to a cup; two cups to a pint; two pints to a quart; four quarts to a gallon; and four gallons to a bucket. Thus, in a bucket of sand, there are nearly two million particles! Now, think of all of the sand on all of the seashores of all of the oceans of the earth! Now consider that all those seashores are just a line on the surface of the earth! How many particles would that be?? Now think of millions of earths like this, and then consider that would not even be a beginning to the number of His creations!!!

All of these worlds were created by God through Jesus Christ. See Ephesians 3:9. So the Savior is the creator of all the worlds. Although he worked out the great atonement on this earth on which we live, He is also not only the creator but also the Savior of all the worlds. In the great vision seen by Joseph Smith and Martin Harris, recorded in the D&C 76, they said,

> *And now, after the many testimonies which have been given of him, this is the testimony, last of all which we give of him: That he lives For we saw him, even on the right hand of God; and we heard the voice bearing record that he is the Only Begotten of the Father—That by him, and through him, and of him, the worlds are and were created, and the inhabitants thereof are begotten sons and daughters unto God.* (D&C 76:22-24)

The preface to that part of D&C 76 explains that "the inhabitants of many worlds are begotten sons and daughters unto God through the atonement of Jesus Christ."

So this earth is unique among all the creations of God as that world to which the Great Jehovah came in mortal sojourn to take upon himself the responsibility to pay to the demands of justice the full price of retribution for all of the sins that have ever been committed or that will ever be committed by all the children of our Father in Heaven in all the infinite number of worlds that they have populated, or will yet live upon! Why did the Savior come to this earth rather than to any other? We are told in D&C 88:6 that He descended below *all things*. If there had been an earth more wicked than this, we would imagine that he would have gone to that world to atone for the sins of humanity in order to have descended below all things.

In speaking to Enoch on one occasion, the Lord made this definitive statement:

> *Wherefore, I can stretch forth mine hands and hold all the creations which I have made; and mine eye can pierce them also, and among all the workmanship of mine hands there has not been so great wickedness as among thy brethren.* (Moses 7:36)

So, by the Lord's own statement, this earth on which we dwell is the most wicked of all the worlds. We have the distinction of living among the greatest evil in the universe. What, then, are we doing here?? The Lord's purpose is to wrest this world from the grasp of Satan and to redeem it as a celestial kingdom, to become His own residence. Nephi's brother, Jacob, tells us in 2 Nephi 2:11 that there must be an opposition in all things. Thus, I suppose that the Lord has called to come to this earth, especially in these last days, those spirits that are sufficiently righteous, faithful, obedient and intelligent and powerful enough to overcome the great evil that is here and help to prepare the earth for the triumphal return of the Savior at the beginning of the Millennium. You are undoubtedly among those chosen ones. It's an honor for me to have the privilege to communicate with you.

—Gramps

WHY IS THERE OPPOSITION IN MORTALITY?

Dear Gramps,

If we are punished for our own sins and not for Adam's (or Eve's) transgression, then why is it that we must work by the sweat of our brows and in sorrow bear children?

Chip

Dear Chip,

When Adam and Eve lived in the Garden of Eden, the earth was in a state to which it will be returned during the millennium. Eve, being deceived by Satan, partook of the forbidden fruit and therefore would be cast out of the Garden of Eden. Adam, realizing that it would be better to partake of the forbidden fruit and remain with Eve so that they could procreate and begin the race of earth's inhabitants rather than remain in the Garden alone, knowingly partook of the fruit so that the human family could follow.

It is essential to God's plan that Adam's children work out their salvation in a telestial sphere where Satan has power so that they could learn to overcome opposition and choose by their own volition to follow God in an environment of adversity. The opposition we experience in mortality— temptation, pain, suffering, disappointment, the necessity to labor to overcome an adverse environment— was not designed as a punishment but rather as a blessing. Our task is to become like the Savior. In fact, the Lord has commanded, *Be ye therefore perfect, even as your Father which is in heaven is perfect.* (Matthew 5:48) In order to do so, we must overcome the world. The Lord has said, *For verily I say unto you, I will that ye should overcome the world; wherefore I will have compassion upon you.* (D&C 64:2)

Mortality in the telestial kingdom was not given as a punishment to man because of the acts of Adam and Eve, but as an opportunity to develop and exhibit faith in the Lord, Jesus Christ, and to live by every word that proceedeth forth from the mouth of God. In mortality we will be punished for our own disobedience and rewarded for our own righteousness, and to him who overcomes the greater opposition will come the greater reward.

—Gramps

WHY DO THEY SERVE HERBAL TEA IN THE TEMPLE CAFETERIAS?

Gramps,

I have a question for you. We as Mormons have the Word of Wisdom to guide us. I am talking about the tea and coffee part. My family does not have a problem with that, we all obey that commandment. My question is why do they have herbal tea in the temples to serve and some members think it all right to drink the tea made with herbs. I have been taught that even the very appearance of things wrong we shouldn't do or partake of. It is really hard to try to explain this to converts that are going to the temple and have been taught that they have to stop drinking tea and coffee so they can become a member of the church. I am looking forward for an answer. Thanks,

Coastal Girl

Dear Coastal Girl,

Many herbs and plants have been provided by the Lord to be used for restoring health. Both frankincense and myrrh, given by the Wise Men to Jesus at his birth, are oils distilled from herbs. At the time of General Moroni, about 72 B.C., the Book of Mormon account mentions the beneficial effects of plants and roots in controlling fevers—

> *And there were some who died with fevers, which at some seasons of the year were very frequent in the land—but not so much so with fevers, because of the excellent qualities of the many plants and roots which God had prepared to remove the cause of diseases, to which men were subject by the nature of the climate.* (Alma 46:40)

Also, in the Doctrine & Covenants we are counseled to use herbs for medicinal purposes—

> *And whosoever among you are sick, and have not faith to be healed, but believe, shall be nourished with all tenderness, with herbs and mild food, and that not by the hand of an enemy.* (D&C 42:43)

And the Lord states that herbs "are made for the benefit and use of man."

> *Yea, and the herb, and the good things which come of the earth, whether for food or for raiment, or for houses, or for barns, or for orchards, or for gardens, or for vineyards;*
> *Yea, all things which come of the earth, in the season thereof, are made for the benefit and the use of man, both to please the eye and to gladden the heart.* (D&C 59:17-18)

It is well and appropriate to keep ourselves from the very appearance of evil. But, of course, partaking of the good things of the earth is not evil. Perhaps we could help the newer members to see and rejoice in the goodness of God in providing for "the benefit of man"…"both to please the eye and to gladden the heart."

If we were to have a cup of herbal tea in a public restaurant, where it would be served in a regular tea cup, it could be assumed by others that we were drinking conventional tea. In such a case it might be prudent to avoid drinking the herbal tea to prevent the possibility of giving others a wrong impression. But no one could ever assume that regular tea would be served in the temple, and those who go there are undoubtedly mature enough in the gospel not to think otherwise.

—Gramps

WHAT DO THE SCRIPTURES SAY ABOUT BODY PIERCING?

Hi Gramps,

My mother says she once found a reference in the scriptures that spoke against body piercing. She has not been able to locate it again. Could you help? Thanks

Leonard

Dear Leonard,

Perhaps your mother was referring to scriptures that indicate that our bodies are sacred vessels, and so it may be inferred that they should be treated with reverence, rather than being mutilated or adorned with unnatural affectations. Paul exclaims in I Corinthians,

> *What? know ye not that your body is the temple of the Holy Ghost which is in you, which ye have of God, and ye are not your own? For ye are bought with a price: therefore glorify God in your body, and in your spirit, which are God's.* (1 Corinthians 6:19-20)

Paul explains that through the infinite suffering of the Son, we have been purchased with a great price, and therefore belong to Him who purchased us; that our physical bodies are indeed temples in which the Holy Ghost may dwell; and that we are to glorify God not only in spirit (by the way we think, speak and act), but also in our bodies (by treating them with the utmost honor and respect).

Our bodies are sacred because they are fashioned in the very image and likeness of the Great and Eternal God, the Creator of the universe; and because we are the offspring (of the same race of beings) of God, and therefore have within us the potential to mature to the stature of our Eternal Parent. Again Paul says,

> *The Spirit itself beareth witness with our spirit, that we are the children of God: And if children, then heirs; heirs of God, and joint-heirs with Christ; if so be that we suffer with him, that we may be also glorified together.* (Romans (8:16-17)

There is no doubt that it is offensive in the sight of God to puncture the body in order to make a display of vanity, or to mutilate the body in any way, such as defacing it with tattoos, with wild and unnatural hair colorings, etc.

Isaiah prophesies of the displeasure of the Lord with the proud and vain, who so adorn their bodies—

Moreover the LORD saith, Because the daughters of Zion are haughty, and walk with stretched forth necks and wanton eyes, walking and mincing as they go, and making a tinkling with their feet: Therefore the Lord will smite with a scab the crown of the head of the daughters of Zion, and the LORD will discover their secret parts. In that day the Lord will take away the bravery of their tinkling ornaments about their feet, and their cauls, and their round tires like the moon, The chains, and the bracelets, and the mufflers, The bonnets, and the ornaments of the legs, and the headbands, and the tablets, and the earrings, The rings, and nose jewels, The changeable suits of apparel, and the mantles, and the wimples, and the crisping pins, The glasses, and the fine linen, and the hoods, and the vails. And it shall come to pass, that instead of sweet smell there shall be stink; and instead of a girdle a rent; and instead of well set hair baldness; and instead of a stomacher a girding of sackcloth; and burning instead of beauty. Thy men shall fall by the sword, and thy mighty in the war. And her gates shall lament and mourn; and she being desolate shall sit upon the ground. (Isaiah 3:16-26)

If the Lord has instructed us that we should have respect for and care for our bodies internally—

And, again, strong drinks are not for the belly, but for the washing of your bodies. And again, tobacco is not for the body, neither for the belly, and is not good for man...And again, hot drinks are not for the body or belly. (D&C 89:7-9)

Is it not reasonable that the exterior of our bodies should receive the same care and respect?

Not only do the scriptures speak of the sacred nature of the human body, but the General Authorities in our own day have been unequivocal on the subject. Just to cite one reference from Elder Mark E. Petersen—

The human body is as sacred as any building ever erected, whether temple or tabernacle itself. It provides a mortal home for our own spirits, which are divine, the very offspring of God, and it may be a resting place for the Holy Spirit to which all followers of God are entitled...Can temples made with stone and brick be any more sacred than the human temple? (Mark E. Petersen, *A Faith to Live By*, pp. 311-12)

—Gramps

WHAT IS THE HOUSE OF ESAU?

Dear Gramps,

I have a number of people ask me the question "What is the House of Esau?" and I wonder if there is any special relevance this statement might have to missionary work other than we are to take it to the world? I would appreciate your opinion, if you have time to give it.

Thanks so much,

Karilin

Dear Karilin,

As you know, although Esau was the older brother, Jacob received the blessing of the firstborn, and became heir to the blessings of Abraham through his father, Isaac. Esau married two Hittite women, "*which were a grief of mind unto Isaac and to Rebekah.*" (Gen. 26:35)

Because of the disobedience of Esau his name was changed to Edom and his descendants are known as Edomites. The Arabic nations have descended from Edom and the Jewish nations from Jacob and Judah. Dire predictions against the Edomites were made by the Lord's prophets.

> *Thus saith the Lord GOD concerning Edom; We have heard a rumour from the LORD, and an ambassador is sent among the heathen, Arise ye, and let us rise up against her in battle. Behold, I have made thee small among the heathen: thou art greatly despised. The pride of thine heart hath deceived thee, thou that dwellest in the clefts of the rock, whose habitation is high; that saith in his heart, Who shall bring me down to the ground? Though thou exalt thyself as the eagle, and though thou set thy nest among the stars, thence will I bring thee down, saith the LORD.* (Obadiah 1:1-4)

> *And the house of Jacob shall be a fire, and the house of Joseph a flame, and the house of Esau for stubble, and they shall kindle in them, and devour them; and there shall not be any remaining of the house of Esau; for the LORD hath spoken it.* (Obadiah 1:18)

Elder Bruce R. McConkie has written that

...through the lineage of Jacob, God sent those valiant spirits, those noble and great ones, who in his infinite wisdom and foreknowledge he knew would be inclined to serve him. Through Esau came those spirits of lesser valiance and devotion.

Hence, in the very nature of things, many of Jacob's seed were righteous in this life, and many of Esau's were wicked, causing Malachi to say in the Lord's name, some fifteen hundred years later, that God loved the house of Jacob and hated the house of Esau. (Mal. 1:2-3; see also Bruce R. McConkie, *Doctrinal New Testament Commentary,* Vol.2, p.277)

According to Brigham Young, the House of Esau comprises the gentile nations. (*Discourses of Brigham Young* 6:344) The promise has been that in our day the gospel is first taken to the gentiles and then to the Jews. So the House of Jacob, manifested principally through the House of Ephraim, are acting as saviors on Mt. Zion to the descendants of Esau. President Young further stated that

> We are called to be Saints, to be the chosen people of the Lord Almighty, to be the saviors of the children of men, to gather the house of Israel, and save the house of Esau." (*Journal of Discourses,* Vol.12, p.118)

—Gramps

WHY DOES A TETANUS SHOT HURT SO MUCH?

Dear Gramps,
Why does a tetanus shot hurt so much? Thanks!
Kristi

Dear Kristi,
Anterior cingulate (AC) has been a consistent area of activation in the pain neuroimaging studies. Electrophysiological studies in anesthetized rats and conditioned rabbits revealed that a high proportion of AC neurons are activated with noxious stimulation.

So there you have it. A tetanus shot is without doubt a noxious stimulation. When you get the shot the anterior cingulate neurons go to work. That really hurts.
—Gramps

WHY DO NOT WOMEN HOLD THE PRIESTHOOD?

Dear Gramps,
Since both of my grandpas are dead, I hope you might help. What is a good explanation for non-members about women not holding the priesthood in our church? Thanks in advance for your time and wisdom.
Regards,
Russ

Dear Russ,

Perhaps there are many sisters within the Church as well that ask the same question. There are some who think that women are second class citizens because they don't hold the priesthood. Nothing could be further from the truth. The family is the basic unit in the Church, and it is organized, as are the other units, along the lines of priesthood authority.

The husband and wife form an equal partnership, although, by the very nature of their beings, their responsibilities are not the same. To the mother God has given the responsibility for the physical birth and for the training and upbringing of the children; to the father God has given the responsibility for the spiritual birth and for the training and upbringing of the children. No more could a woman baptize a child than could a man bear a child. In this relationship, the father, by virtue of his priesthood presides over the home; but the authority given to the father in the home is not related to the concept of authority in the world; and perhaps this is the source of much of the misunderstanding and discontent about this concept of authority.

The principles of priesthood authority and influence as announced in D&C 121:41-42 are persuasion, long-suffering, gentleness, meekness, love unfeigned and kindness. These are the principles that the husband and father is authorized to use by virtue of his priesthood. As you consider, for instance, a mother with a newborn child, it becomes immediately apparent that these qualities are the natural characteristics of our sisters. It might be suggested that they do not need to be ordained to the qualities that they already inherently possess.

Since the greatest degree of learning and the greatest character set takes place in children at their very earliest age, the mother, who bears the children, is also primarily responsible for their nurturing. So to the man is given responsibility to conduct the affairs of the church outside the home.

In the celestial kingdom, exaltation is proffered only to husbands and wives together. In this exalted state the priesthood is shared equally by both partners. Yet here, preserving the order of heaven, the husband presides, and I would assume that the wife would continue to provide the greatest influence. Paul tells us that—*neither is the man without the woman, neither the woman without the man, in the Lord.* (1 Corinthians 11:11)

—Gramps

CAN YOU TELL ME WHY THE LORD WOULD REVEAL HIS WILL TO ME, ALTHOUGH I AM NOT YET BAPTIZED?

Dear Gramps:

My daughter, son in law and wife are LDS members. I haven't been baptized yet, but I have a troubling question. My daughter gave birth to a preemie baby, Jona Scott, 1 pound 12 oz. The last blessing she had the brother said the baby would be born in 3 days, and would be a great leader. While I was sleeping last night I was awakened suddenly and told to pray for little Ben, and little Ben and Jona were one and the same. Can you give me any idea why this would come to me and what it might mean. I have a feeling that Jona will make it through despite the odds.

Don

Dear Don,

I would imagine that such an inspiration would come to you because of a number of circumstances: 1) You undoubtedly are living a life of sufficient righteousness that the Lord would speak to you. 2) You are sufficiently sensitive to the voice of the Spirit to recognize its influence. 3) You recognize the power of the prayer of faith. The fact that you have a feeling that Jona will make it through despite the odds is an indication of your faith in the Lord and that He will hear your prayers.

In such circumstances we must believe that the Lord is in control, and that His will shall be accomplished. So whatever the outcome we may be able to thank the Lord for his blessings upon us. It may be to sustain the life of an infant, or it may be to give us understanding and strength to accept his will, whatever it may be.

There is no doubt that the Lord loves you and your family, and will provide the influence that will clarify your path before you so that you may have the faith, testimony and confidence to follow His will in all things.

—Gramps

IS CREMATION AN ACCEPTABLE PRACTICE?

Dear Gramps;
I realize that LDS have been counseled against cremation in all ages, but some, like my in-laws, did it anyway. In some cultures and areas of the world it is the accepted and expected practice. With low budget funerals in the $6,000 range, how is a widow(er) of little means to honor this decree?
Catherine

Dear Catherine,
Although the Church takes no official position on the manner of the disposition of the body after death, as you have indicated, the Brethren counsel that consignment to the earth is proper and appropriate. The body, of course, is a sacred vessel, being formed in the very image of God, and as the tabernacle of the spirit, which is a child of God.

The following counsel is given in the Priesthood Bulletin, 1980—

The Church of Jesus Christ of Latter-day Saints counsels its members to bury their dead in the earth to return dust to dust, unless the law of the country requires cremation. However, the decision whether to bury or cremate the body is left to the family of the deceased, taking into account any laws governing the matter.

The cost of funeral services and burial vary widely, accommodating both the means of the affluent and of the indigent. Thus almost every budget can somehow be accommodated. It would be wise when such needs arose to counsel with one's bishop, who would give compassionate consideration to both the interests and the limited means of the family of the deceased.

—Gramps

WHY DID JESUS DRINK WINE?

Dear Gramps,
I know that the Word of Wisdom was given to us through Joseph Smith to keep our bodies clean and free from disease. I also know that wine and strong drink are not good for the body. If this is so, why did Jesus drink wine?
Kristi

Dear Kristi,

I know of no reference in the scriptures of the Savior drinking wine, except in preparing the sacrament for his disciples. The question is, what was the "wine" that was used in the sacrament?

Smith and Sjodahl, in *Doctrine and Covenants Commentary,* Sec. 89, p. 572, report the following:

> The use of "pure wine" in the Sacrament is permitted. But what is "pure wine" if not the pure juice of the grape, before it has been adulterated by the process of fermentation? No fewer than thirteen Hebrew and Greek terms are rendered in our Bible by the word "wine." There is the pure grape juice, and a kind of grape syrup, the thickness of which made it necessary to mingle water with it previously to drinking. (Prov. 9:2, 5) There was a wine made strong and inebriating by the addition of drugs, such as myrrh, mandragora, and opiates. (Prov. 23:30; Isa. 5:22) Of the pure wine which was diluted with water, or milk, Wisdom invites her friends to drink freely. (Prov. 9:2, 5) There was also 'wine on the lees,' which is supposed to have been 'preserves' or 'jellies'. (Isa. 25:6) The 'pure wine' is not an intoxicating, but a harmless liquid."

Also, Elder John A. Widtsoe in *Evidences and Reconciliations*, p. 79, had this to say:

> A sacrament means a solemn, sacred religious ordinance. There are many of them. The sacrament as understood by the Church, and discussed here, is the partaking of bread and water (or unfermented wine) as emblems of the body and blood of the Lord Jesus Christ.

When the sacrament was instituted by Joseph Smith at the beginning of the restoration, the sacramental prayers were given by revelation. The prayers refer to bread and wine as the sacramental emblems. (See D&C 20:77-79) However, in a subsequent revelation Joseph received the following instruction,

> *For, behold, I say unto you, that it mattereth not what ye shall eat or what ye shall drink when ye partake of the sacrament, if it so be that ye do it with an eye single to my glory—remembering unto the Father my body which was laid down for you, and my blood which was shed for the remission of your sins*
>
> *Wherefore, a commandment I give unto you, that you shall not purchase wine neither strong drink of your enemies;*
>
> *Wherefore, you shall partake of none except it is made new among you; yea, in this my Father's kingdom which shall be built up on the earth.* (D&C 27:2-4)

On this authority water was substituted for wine in the sacrament.
—Gramps

WERE ADAM AND EVE IN THE GARDEN OF EDEN AWARE OF THE PLAN OF SALVATION?

Hi Gramps;

Once again I come to you with a question—I am so glad you are here to ask. Did Adam and Eve know of the plan, and eat of the fruit because of the plan, or was it a situation where they did not know and chose to? I had a gentleman from the Jehovah Witnesses challenge me to find the scripture that indicated one or the other. I enjoy searching, but do not know where to look, and I need to know, too. Thanks.

Patti

Dear Patti,

Before the fall Adam and Eve were immortal, terrestrial beings, living on a terrestrial earth. According to Elder Bruce R. McConkie,

> When the Lord created this earth, it was in a terrestrial state, an Edenic state, a paradisiacal state; death had not then entered the world. Adam and Eve and all created things were in an immortal state. (*Doctrinal New Testament Commentary*, Vol.3, p.367)

They undoubtedly knew of the plan of salvation. They had been instructed by the Lord. However, they possessed their free wills and had their agency. Eve was tempted by Satan and succumbed to the temptation. However, Adam resisted the temptation, but knowingly partook of the forbidden fruit in order to fulfill the Lord's plan

> *And Adam was not deceived, but the woman being deceived was in the transgression.* (1 Timothy 2:14)

—Gramps

IS EATING MEAT AGAINST THE WORD OF WISDOM?

Dear Gramps,

As a fairly new member of the church, I've always wondered about the Word of Wisdom as it relates to the eating of meat. As I understand it, it sounds to me like we should be vegetarians, that meat is for times of famine. Since we, at least in the United States, have such an abundance of food, other than meat, at our disposal, shouldn't we be refraining from eating meat?

Larmour

Dear Larmour,

To consider the topic of eating meat, we need to examine D&C Section 89 and other related scriptures very carefully. The kernel of the question is found in verses 12 and 13.

> Yea, flesh also of beasts and of the fowls of the air, I, the Lord, have ordained for the use of man with thanksgiving; nevertheless they are to be used sparingly;
>
> And it is pleasing unto me that they should not be used, only in times of winter, or of cold, or famine.

In verse 12 we have the positive statement that the flesh of beasts and of the fowls of the air are ordained for the use of man, although they are to be used sparingly. That does not sound like we should be vegetarians. Verse 13, as it is written, suggests that meat should not be used *except* in times of winter, cold or famine. The dependent clause, *only in times of winter, or of cold, or famine,* appears as an exception to the verb by virtue of the comma following the word *used.*

It is rather interesting to note that this comma did not appear in the early editions of the Doctrine and Covenants. In fact it was first introduced in the edition dated 17 Dec. 1921, when the Doctrine and Covenants was first divided into columns. If we look at verse 13 as it appeared before the 1921 edition, it reads,

> And it is pleasing unto me that they should not be used only in times of winter, or of cold, or famine.

Now, instead of a dependent clause, the last phrase becomes the direct object of the sentence, with the intent that winter, cold or famine are not the only times that they, the flesh of beasts and of the fowls of the air, should be used, but implying that they should be used at other seasons, as well.

Now let's look at verses 14 and 15.

> All grain is ordained for the use of man and of beasts, to be the staff of life, not only for man but for the beasts of the field, and the fowls of heaven, and all wild animals that run or creep on the earth;
>
> And these hath God made for the use of man only in times of famine and excess of hunger.

Verse 14 says that grain is ordained for the use of man, the beasts of the field, the fowls of heaven and all wild animals. And in verse 15,

> And <u>these</u> hath God made for the use of man only in times of famine and excess of hunger.

The antecedent of the pronoun, *these,* could refer to the entire phrase— beasts, fowls and wild animals—or it could refer only to the latter—wild animals, since beasts and fowls represent one category of meat and wild animals another. That it does refer only to the latter is demonstrated in D&C 46:19:

> *For, behold, the beasts of the field and the fowls of the air, and that which cometh of the earth, is ordained for the use of man for food and for raiment, and that he might have in abundance.*

If the beasts of the field and the fowls of the air are ordained for food for man, that he might have in abundance, it is logical that the pronoun, *these*, in D&C 89:15 refers only to the wild animals that man should eat only in times of great necessity. That concept is also consistent with D&C 49:21, which says;

> *And wo be unto man that sheddeth blood or that wasteth flesh and hath no need.*

Beasts of the field refer to domesticated animals as opposed to wild animals. Enos, in Enos 1:20 refers to the idolatrous and blood-thirsty Lamanites feeding upon wild animals, or *beasts of prey,* as filthiness.

Elders Bruce R. McConkie and Mark E. Peterson in speaking of the Word of Wisdom, both indicate that abstinence from eating meat is not ordained of God.

> Those who command that men should not eat meat, are not ordained of God, such counsel being listed by Paul as an evidence of apostasy. God has created "meats," he says, "to be received with thanksgiving of them which believe and know the truth." (1 Tim. 4:3; see also Bruce R. McConkie, *Mormon Doctrine*, p.846)

> It will be noted that the Lord in the Word of Wisdom cautions against the excessive use of meats. But the Lord also warns against those who say that we should eat no meat at all. (Mark E. Peterson, *A Word of Wisdom*, p. 16)

—Gramps

WHAT WAS THE PURPOSE OF THE TABERNACLE THAT MOSES USED AMONG THE ISRAELITES?

Dear Gramps,

I have a question...What did the Israelites do in the tabernacle? They only had the Aaronic Priesthood and could not receive the temple endowment. I read that the High Priests went in only once a year. I need more information. We really enjoy your efforts as we study the Gospel Doctrine lessons. Thank you.

Pat & Jerry

Dear Pat and Jerry,

Moses tried to prepare his people to live lives of worthiness sufficient for them to receive and administer in the higher ordinances of the gospel, but because of their disbelief and wickedness the higher priesthood was taken from them, and they were left only with authority to administer in the outward ordinances. However, Moses and subsequent prophets retained the Melchizedek priesthood and administered in the ordinances thereof.

No vicarious work for the dead, however, was performed until after the redemptive sacrifice of the Savior. During the period between His death and resurrection He opened the doors to the preaching of the gospel to the departed spirits, and initiated vicarious temple work. Hence Paul's statement in speaking to the church at Corinth to convince them of the reality of the resurrection,

> *Else what shall they do which are baptized for the dead, if the dead rise not at all? why are they then baptized for the dead?* (1 Corinthians 15:29)

President Joseph Fielding Smith, in *Answers to Gospel Questions*, Vol.2, p.80, answered your question in this way:

> The work done in the wilderness and later in the temple in Jerusalem was confined to ordinances for the living, as certain scripture will clearly show in both the Old and the New Testaments. Many of the ancient prophets held the keys of the priesthood, which enabled them to perform the ordinances and obtain the necessary blessings to entitle them to a place in the celestial kingdom. And these blessings continued to be given to those who were worthy, and after the resurrection of Christ they came forth to obtain their exaltation in the celestial kingdom.

—Gramps

COMMUNICATION WITH THE SPIRIT WORLD

Dear Gramps,

In this day of new age and learning there is a lot of information on connecting with your spirit and meditation. I have a dear friend that has a spiritual gift to read someone's spirit. She has gone to her bishop and has talked with him about the feelings and insights she has. Her first bishop was very uncomfortable with what she said she could do. Another bishop she had supports her and has given her priesthood blessings about the gift she always has had. Somehow she is able to connect with your spirit and tell you about the talents you have and need to magnify. Some of the

*information that was told to my friend was in her patriarchal blessing. She
was reading a friend's spirit and told her that she has two "entities" that
have clung to her for two years. She explained that entities are people that
have died and have not gone to the spirit world and still try to live their
lives through other people. She also said that you can pick up these entities
at hospitals, bars, and mortuaries. This is one reason why the church tells
us not to go into bars because of the influences of evil that are there. This
probably sounds very strange to you and I know that Heavenly Father
wants us to rely on Him and turn to Him for answers to our problems and
not to rely on human beings that are sensitive to the spirit. I guess my question for you is that: Is it possible for anyone to have been blessed with spiritual gifts such as these that I have told you about? My daughter went to
seminary and asked her seminary teacher about having 'entities' and he
told her he had never heard about them and said it is impossible to have
them attach themselves to you. What can you tell us about this? What about
having spiritual gifts and helping other people with this gift? Thank you for
your help in which we are trying to get answers for!*
Mildred

Dear Mildred,

There is no doubt about the existence of sprits beyond the grave. All
who have lived in mortality continue to live in the spirit world. We are told
by Brigham Young that the spirit world is on the earth and in our surroundings. (*Journal of Discourses*, 3:369) There is also no doubt that under certain conditions departed spirits can communicate with mortals. There
further is no doubt that there are both righteous and evil spirits in the spirit
world.

We find no scriptural evidence nor counsel of the Brethren that suggests
that we should attempt to communicate directly with departed spirits. There
are recorded instances, however, where both righteous and unrighteous
spirits have communicated with persons living in mortality on the earth.

President Harold B. Lee quoted Parley P. Pratt as follows:

Their kindred spirit, their guardian angels,...hover about them with
the fondest affection, the most anxious solicitude. Spirit communes with
spirit, thought meets thought, soul blends with soul, in all the raptures of
mutual pure and eternal love. In this situation the spiritual organs and if
we could see our spirits, we would know that they have eyes to see, ears
to hear, tongues to speak, and so on are susceptible of converse with Deity,
or of communion with angels, and the spirits of just men made perfect. In
this situation we frequently hold communion with our departed father,
mother, brother, sister, son or daughter, or with the former husband or wife

of our bosom whose affections for us, being rooted and grounded in the eternal elements, issuing from under the sanctuary of love's eternal fountain, can never be lessened or diminished by death, distance of space, or length of years. (*Stand Ye In Holy Places*, p.142-143)

The communication referred to above by Brother Pratt required no intervention of a third party with a "spiritual gift."

There are also attempts by evil spirits to communicate with mortals. Their purpose, being evil, would be only to subvert the plans of the Lord or to compromise the righteousness of the individual. Here is a quote by President Wilford Woodruff:

> One evening, as I fell asleep, I was very much troubled with evil spirits that tried to afflict me; and while laboring to throw off these spirits and their influence, there was another spirit visited me that seemed to have power over the evil spirits, and they departed from me. Before he left me he told me not to grieve because of the departure of Abraham Hoagland Cannon; for the Lord had called him to fill another important mission in the spirit world, as a pure and holy apostle from Zion in the Rocky Mountains—a labor which would not only prove a great benefit to his father's household, but to the Church and kingdom of God on the earth. (*The Discourses of Wilford Woodruff*, p. 292)

President Joseph Fielding Smith has recorded the following:

> There is no satisfactory evidence that the spirits of the departed communicate with mortals through spiritual mediums or any of the means commonly employed for that purpose. Evil spirits, no doubt, act as "familiars" or as "controls" and either personate the spirits of the dead or reveal things supposed to be known only to them and their living friends, in order to lead away the credulous, but those who place themselves under the influence of those powers of darkness have no means by which they can compel the presence of the spirits of the just or induce disclosures from them to the living. They are above and beyond the art of such individuals, and the mediums themselves are frequently the dupes of evil spirits and are thus "deceivers and being deceived." (*Answers to Gospel Questions*, Vol.4, p. 109)

Elder Bruce R. McConkie has also spoken on the subject:

> It is true that some mediums do make contact with spirits during their seances. In most instances, however, such spirits as manifest themselves are probably the demons or devils who were cast out of heaven for rebellion. Such departed spirits as become involved in these spiritualistic orgies would obviously be the spirits of wicked and depraved persons who because of their previous wickedness in mortality had wholly subjected themselves to the dominion of Lucifer. Righteous spirits would have nothing but contempt and pity for the attempts of mediums to make contact with them. (*Mormon Doctrine*, p. 759)

If your friend indeed has a "gift" of contact with the spirit world, I would imagine that it would be for her benefit only, and not to be shared with others. If spirits came to her for the purpose of making contact with any other person, one could rest assured that they would not be righteous spirits with a message from the Lord. Again, Elder Bruce R. McConkie gives this counsel:

> Mediums are witches; they are persons who have so trained and schooled themselves in sorcery and spiritualism that they have ready access to and communion with evil spirits. In modern spiritualism they are the ones who conduct seances and who profess to call back the dead and receive messages from them. In the main, of course, the messages received are from devils and not from the departed dead. (*Mormon Doctrine,* p. 473)

I think your friend is wise in seeking counsel and direction from her priesthood leaders. If she lives according to the principles of the gospel and follows the counsel of her leaders, I'm sure that she will be blessed with the guidance necessary to avoid associations with the emissaries of the adversary.

—Gramps

WHAT HAPPENS TO BODIES THAT ARE DESTROYED AFTER DEATH?

Dear Gramps,

What happens if a member of the church is cremated instead of being buried? What happens if a person dies and that member is not buried or even cremated but dies on top of the ground or in the water? Thanks, Gramps; I await your explanation.

John

Dear John,

I assume that your question relates to whether or not a person can be resurrected if his body is somehow destroyed at death, rather than being preserved and buried the conventional manner. The Lord is all powerful. When He made the earth, He merely had to command the elements and they obeyed his command. You might review Chapter 4 of Abraham to see how God ordered the creation and the elements obeyed. Here is one verse that demonstrates how it was done:

> *And the Gods ordered the expanse, so that it divided the waters which*
> *were under the expanse from the waters which were above the expanse;*
> *and it was so, even as they ordered.* (Abraham 4:7)

So if God can speak and the elements obey, surely He can command the
elements that have made up the physical body of a person to be reunited and
come together as a living, immortal person. In the words of Patriarch Eldred
G. Smith,

> Even though this body goes into the grave and is decomposed, or if it
> is burned, or if it is lost at sea, no matter what is done to this body after
> death, the elements of this body are elements of the earth and cannot be
> destroyed. (Eldred G. Smith, *BYU Speeches*, March 10, 1964, p.3)

—Gramps

WHERE ARE THE LOST TEN TRIBES?

Dear Gramps,
What are your thoughts on the whereabouts of the lost ten tribes? My
mother-in-law thinks that they were taken away on a continent that was
once part of the earth??
Thalia

Dear Thalia,
You've just asked the easiest question in the world to answer: Where
are the lost ten tribes? Answer: I don't know! And neither does anyone else,
or they wouldn't be lost. Theories abound as to where they might be, but no
one knows.

How did they get lost in the first place? In 721 B.C. the ten tribes, ruled
by Rehoboam, and known as the Kingdom of Israel, (as opposed to the
remaining two tribes in Jerusalem who were ruled by Jeroboam and known
as the Kingdom of Judah) were carried captive into Assyria by King
Shalmaneser. Years later, when they were finally released from captivity,
they did not return to Palestine to the land of their inheritance, but departed
into the north and disappeared. President Joseph Fielding Smith has written:

> To this day the ten tribes are lost to the world. As they journeyed to
> the north many of their number straggled and fell behind and mingled with
> the peoples in the lands through which they passed, but the main body
> continued on their journey and were hidden by the hand of the Lord.
> (Joseph Fielding Smith, *The Restoration of All Things*, p. 131)

From the words of the prophets recorded in the scriptures, we learn a bit more. Nephi, somewhere between 12 and 30 years after he left Jerusalem, reported:

> *There are many who are already lost from the knowledge of those who are at Jerusalem. Yea, the more part of all the tribes have been led away; and they are scattered to and fro upon the isles of the sea; and whither they are none of us knoweth, save that we know that they have been led away.* (1 Nephi 22:4)

This scripture suggests that, being "scattered to and fro," they may not exist as a defined nation but rather exist as individuals among other nations, as Judah has done until a nation was defined for them after the Second World War. But the Savior, speaking to the Nephites after his resurrection, assures us that at that time they existed as a body—

> *But now I go unto the Father, and also to show myself unto the lost tribes of Israel, for they are not lost unto the Father, for he knoweth whither he hath taken them.* (3 Nephi 17:4)

We learn from the scriptures that the lost Ten Tribes will one day return and be recognized for who they are. Nephi again tells us,

> *And it shall come to pass that the Jews shall have the words of the Nephites, and the Nephites shall have the words of the Jews; and the Nephites and the Jews shall have the words of the lost tribes of Israel; and the lost tribes of Israel shall have the words of the Nephites and the Jews.* (2 Nephi 29:13)

The Savior revealed to the Nephites that at some future time the redemptive work would be introduced among the tribes that have been led away. (See 3 Nephi 21:26)

To Joseph Smith in D&C 133:26-34, the Lord revealed some rather specific information concerning the return of the ten tribes:

> *And they who are in the north countries shall come in remembrance before the Lord; and their prophets shall hear his voice, and shall no longer stay themselves; and they shall smite the rocks, and the ice shall flow down at their presence.*
>
> *And an highway shall be cast up in the midst of the great deep.*
>
> *Their enemies shall become a prey unto them,*
>
> *And in the barren deserts there shall come forth pools of living water; and the parched ground shall no longer be a thirsty land.*
>
> *And they shall bring forth their rich treasures unto the children of Ephraim, my servants.*
>
> *And the boundaries of the everlasting hills shall tremble at their presence.*

And there shall they fall down and be crowned with glory, even in Zion, by the hands of the servants of the Lord, even the children of Ephraim.

And they shall be filled with songs of everlasting joy.

Behold, this is the blessing of the everlasting God upon the tribes of Israel, and the richer blessing upon the head of Ephraim and his fellows.

The rather enigmatic statements, *and they shall smite the rocks, and the ice shall flow down at their presence,* and *an highway shall be cast up in the midst of the great deep,* both suggest that when the ten tribes return they shall be in a body. They were apparently in a body when John the Revelator was sent to minister to them. The question is, where are they now and what has been their state during the 2000-year interval between the advent of John among them and their eventual return to be crowned with glory in Zion? On this the scriptures are silent and their identity to date has not been revealed nor discovered. It is an idle and unprofitable exercise to speculate as to where they are now, whether they live together as a nation or whether they will be gathered from among the nations; whether they have lived for 2000 years with the knowledge of their scriptures, or whether their scriptures will be rediscovered as were the scriptures of the Nephites; whether the highway to be cast up in the midst of the great deep shall miraculously emerge from the ocean, or whether it will be *cast up* as the 26-mile highway over Lake Pontchartrain was cast up; whether the living pools of water will be the result of geological or climatic changes, or will be the result of developments in irrigation.

But one thing is certain: When all these things occur, we shall recognize that they represent the fulfillment of prophecy, and our faith shall be confirmed. Great things are in store!

—Gramps

TESTIMONY BEARING BY SMALL CHILDREN

Dear Gramps,

I am concerned that my eleven-year-old son is dead set against bearing his testimony in public, not even in Primary. He gives wonderful talks and has no fear of speaking in public, he just doesn't want to bear his testimony. I suspect this has to do with his feeling that his testimony isn't strong enough to matter. I've tried to teach him that our testimonies grow when we share them. Is there anything else that I can do to help him? I'm afraid that

this might have a negative influence on his entire life. Thank you for your column. You give some wonderfully inspired answers.
Lorrie

Dear Lorrie,

There are a number of reasons why young people may be reticent to bear their testimonies. A person may be confident in presenting a prepared talk, but be very concerned about speaking extemporaneously. It's also true, as you indicate, that many young people are not sure that they have "testimonies" of the truthfulness of the gospel, although they believe what they have been taught. Others may be unsure of their own beliefs or confused about just what constitutes a testimony.

Perhaps someone could assign your son to give a talk in sacrament meeting on fast day with a defined subject such as "What I believe about the Savior," or "Joseph Smith was a prophet of God," or "What the scriptures mean to me," etc., etc.

I would also suggest that we may do more harm than good by applying too much pressure for a young person to bear his testimony. If for any reason he is not ready to do so, his objections may form barriers in his mind that would outlast his feelings of unpreparedness.

Perhaps you could suggest to him that he prepare to express himself as a witness of the goodness of God to him, and of the feelings with which the Lord has blessed him concerning the truthfulness of the plan of salvation by asking the Lord each day to give him the strength and desire to be His witness to others who could benefit from his expression of faith. Then express confidence in him that when he is ready you know that he will do well and that you will support him. Then let him know that it will be his decision as to when he should respond to the feelings within him and declare himself publicly. He will gain much more by following the dictates of his own conscience than by responding to the pressures imposed by a loving and concerned parent.

—Gramps

WHO WROTE THE BOOKS
OF THE NEW TESTAMENT?

Dear Gramps,

In the LDS version of the King James Bible, there is listed at the end of the different books, the supposed author—these authors do not conform to LDS beliefs.

Example: the Book of Hebrews was written by Paul as stated by Joseph Smith. (see Bible Dictionary) Yet at the end of Hebrews it states that Timothy wrote the book. Are these listed authors just part of the King James manuscript? Or is there some other reason they are listed?

Doug

Dear Doug,

The authorship attributed to Hebrews by bible scholars is somewhat uncertain, although it is generally accredited to Paul. It was not uncommon for Paul to have others write his epistles for him. For instance, Paul identifies himself as the author of First Corinthians in verse 1. At the end of the epistle we find that it was written by no less than four people—Stephanas, Fortunatus, Archaicus and Timotheus (Timothy). Paul's second epistle to the Corinthians was written by Titus and Lucas. The epistle to the Ephesians, again identified in the first verse as being from Paul, was written by Tychicus. So it is not surprising that Timothy is cited as the writer of Hebrews. The only problem is that Paul did not identify himself in the first in the epistle.

Timothy was Paul's companion while he was a prisoner in Rome, where the epistle was apparently written. One possibility is that Paul dictated the epistle to Timothy, who added his name at the end as the scribe. Another possibility is that Timothy used his own phraseology to express to the Hebrews Paul's ideas. Sidney B. Sperry suggests the following:

> In view of all the facts thus presented, the author believes along with many other writers ancient and modern, that Paul was the author responsible for the ideas and doctrines of the Epistle to the Hebrews, but that he was not the actual writer who was responsible for its literary form. Possibly the subscription to the Epistle is correct; Timothy may have written it. But Origen may have been right when he said, "Who wrote the Epistle God only knows certainly." (Sidney B. Sperry, *Paul's Life and Letters*, p. 272)

—Gramps

HOW DO I LOSE WEIGHT
AFTER BEARING A CHILD?

Dear Gramps,

I've been looking for a healthy, relatively easy way to lose a few extra pounds put on after having a baby. I've been hearing a lot about low-carbohydrate diets—Dr. Atkins New Revolutionary Diet, Carbohydrate Addict's Diet, Protein Power. Basically, they say you can lose weight by cutting your intake of carbohydrates to about 30 grams a day and you can eat as much non-carb food as you like—meats, eggs, cheese. These are foods with fairly high fat content. Is it possible to lose weight on a plan like this?

Signed, Baby-fat

Dear Baby-fat,

Probably there is no more hype on any subject more than on control of obesity. There must be more than a thousand diet plans on the market, and I suppose that you could lose weight on any of them. There are some things to be cautious about, however. First, one would want to lose weight safely—without deleterious side effects. Secondly, after losing the weight it is vital that some program be employed to keep the excess weight off.

To lose weight safely, it is important not to lose protein tissue, and to maintain appropriate input levels of the micro nutrients, such as vitamins, minerals, trace elements and electrolytes. The loss of protein tissue could be classed as starvation. Great care should be exercised in choosing a diet that will not violate the above conditions.

Weight loss reduces itself to a simple, basic formula—energy in versus energy out. If we consume more energy than we expend, the excess energy is stored as body fat. The human body is a marvelous mechanism for self preservation. Fat tissue is not released into the energy system as long as the fuel from carbohydrates (glucose) is in the blood stream. Therefore, in order to lose weight, carbohydrate consumption must be seriously decreased. When the blood sugar level reaches an appropriately low level, the body will release the lipid tissue into the energy system. When fat tissue is converted to energy, rather than being reduced to glucose, the fuel of carbohydrates, it is reduced to ketones. The burning of ketones for energy has two interesting side effects—it acts as a natural appetite suppressant and it is a mild euphoric. Thus, the body prepares for the absence of food by suppressing the appetite and causing the person to feel more energetic. So, don't be afraid of rapid weight loss diets, as long as they don't rob you of protein tissue or micro nutrients.

When you have reached your ideal weight, if you return to your former eating habits, you will return to your former weight—energy in vs energy out. So it is essential to adopt a new lifestyle: less food! An occasional binge doesn't hurt a thing, but continued overeating does. Here are some general rules of thumb for the number of calories one can consume without gaining weight.

In the first place, about 1200 calories per day are used up in bed rest, principally maintaining the body temperature. The added caloric expenditure depends on the level of activity and on the person's metabolic rate. Since the metabolic rate varies somewhat from person to person, we will assume it be constant. So here is a chart that you can use to determine how many calories you need.

- Light activity—11 times ideal body weight
- Moderate activity—13 times ideal body weight
- Heavy activity—15 times ideal body weight

How to determine ideal body weight:

For women: 100 pounds for the first five feet of height, plus five pounds for each inch of height over five feet. For example, the ideal weight of a 5'4" female would be 120 pounds.

For men: 106 pounds for the first five feet of height, plus six pounds for each inch of height over five feet. For example, the ideal weight of a 5'10' male would be 166 pounds.

A 5'4" female at a moderate activity level would not gain weight consuming about 1560 calories per day.

A 5'10" male at a moderate activity level would not gain weight consuming about 2160 calories per day.

—Gramps

WILL THE SPIRIT ABIDE WITH AN EXCOMMUNICATED PERSON?

Dear Gramps,

I have a question that you may or may not want to answer through your column. What is the status (for lack of a better word) of the Spirit abiding or not abiding with excommunicated persons? I realize that those who are in this situation are worse affected than those never having the gospel. I guess I am asking to what degree the Spirit can abide with those who are excommunicated. If one is working very diligently to gain back his or her membership and blessings, would the Spirit be more inclined to inspire or enlighten the individual? Thank you for your answer.

    Aliece

Dear Aliece,

At baptism the person receives the gift of the Holy Ghost by the laying on of hands. This gift will reveal to the person the truthfulness of sacred things. However, since the Spirit will not dwell in unclean temples (1 Cor. 3:16-17), if a person after baptism violates the covenants he has made he will not enjoy the influence of the Holy Spirit and will be left without inspiration.

    When a person is excommunicated, the blessings received as a member are taken from him, including any priesthood to which he had been ordained and the right to guidance by the Holy Ghost. However, even though a person may have sinned to such a degree that his membership in the Kingdom is revoked, yet he may repent and be forgiven. It must be remembered that excommunication is not used as a punishment, but as a blessing to the person, designed to help the person repent and return to the Lord. Isaiah said,

> *Though your sins be as scarlet, they shall be as white as snow; though they be red like crimson, they shall be as wool.* (Isaiah 1:18)

The Lord is anxious to forgive his wayward children and return them to the fold. Think of the parable of the lost sheep in Matt. 18;11-14.

And further, he has said,

> *Behold, he who has repented of his sins, the same is forgiven, and I, the Lord, remember them no more. By this ye may know if a man repenteth of his sins—behold, he will confess them and forsake them.* (D&C 58:42)

We should be especially attentive to and pray for those who have been excommunicated, that they may not feel ostracized by the society of the saints. Henry Drummond said,

> How many prodigals are kept out of the Kingdom of God by the unlovely characters of those that profess to be within? (*The Greatest Thing in the World*, London and Glasgow, Collins' Clear-Type Press, p. 36)

It would appear that the powers of heaven are available to help the prodigal return, and since *a man may receive the Holy Ghost, and it may descend upon him and not tarry with him,* (D&C 130:23) it would seem that a person who had been excommunicated and was seeking to put his life in order and return to the Kingdom would have as much spiritual help as anyone, perhaps more.

—Gramps

How Can I Help Ease
The Tension At Home?

Hi Gramps,

I so enjoy learning from your letters, but I have something I need help with...kids, who are not members, that are angry, and swear that the one daughter, born of us, is more important than the nephew we raised as a son since he was a baby. Their ages are 24 and 27, but their feelings remain. I want to help the new mom and not make the son angry, what should I do?

Grams

Dear Grams,

Often in our anxiety to do what is right and provide for our loved ones, we tend to feel responsible for their behavior. Indeed we are responsible when they are very young, but as they grow to adulthood they gradually assume more and more of the responsibility for their own behavior. When they reach adulthood they are as responsible for their own behavior as we feel that we are responsible for ours. Their characters are pretty well formed. No doubt characters can and do change, but seldom from the advice of others.

It is sometimes impossible to please all parties with conflicting interests. What then should we do? First, it would be well to let go, in the sense of feeling responsible for their responses to our inputs. Next, in our interactions with them, we must do what in our judgment is for their best good. If we do this without responding with anger when put upon for our actions, but with a smile and a soft answer, the example of our Christ-like behavior will preach the most powerful sermons. Some may be alienated, but if we have behaved properly that is their business. And if we demonstrate when we are treated poorly that we hold no animosity and that we indeed have love and compassion for the person who perceives us as being against them, they will have the best chance of coming to an understanding of our motives and a desire for reconciliation. There is a scripture that says,

> *No power or influence can or ought to be maintained by virtue of the priesthood, only by persuasion, by long-suffering, by gentleness and meekness, and by love unfeigned; By kindness, and pure knowledge, which shall greatly enlarge the soul without hypocrisy, and without guile.* (D&C 121:41-42)

The application of the principles of persuasion, long-suffering, gentleness, meekness, love unfeigned and kindness represent the best ways of exerting power and influence with or without the priesthood.
—Gramps

WHO MAY SET APART AN ELDERS QUORUM PRESIDENT?

Dear Gramps,

According to the <u>General Handbook of Instructions</u> it says that a stake president must set apart an Elders Quorum president because of the keys related to his calling as president. Is there a situation where a counselor in the stake presidency can do this setting apart? And if so, how are the priesthood keys passed down? Thank you.

Brent

Dear Brent,

As you have indicated, the <u>General Handbook of Instructions</u> requires Elders Quorum presidents to be set apart by their stake presidents, and you also cited the reason for this requirement. Counselors to the stake president may set apart counselors to the Elders Quorum presidents, and they may also set apart High Priest Group leaders and their assistants because no transfer of keys of authority is involved. I know of no exceptions to this procedure.

—Gramps

CAN CONVERTS FULLY AND COMPLETELY REPENT?

Dear Gramps,

There are many members that are born into the church, and there are others that were not given the opportunity to be born in the church. These people are converts to the church. My question is about the converts who may have had the worldly things in life, and being that they know the bitter and the sweet there still can be temptations, because of past memories.

How does one say no and mean it, even though deep within yourself you really don't have the strength to say no, because at the very moment you don't care, because you like what you're doing even though it's wrong? What if the only way to say no was to leave that person, how would a person know they can say no the next time if it's been a challenge in the past? Is it better to stay single because of your past? If so that means that one will be without a mate. I don't think anyone wants this so how can one say no and mean it to themselves and to others?

John

Dear John,

It's a new world each day. The difficult experiences of the past give us both knowledge and strength for having overcome them. Nevertheless, temptations continue to come, whether born in the Church or converted at a later age. The challenge is how to overcome temptation.

There are three forces that influence man's behavior: the inspiration of the Holy Spirit, the temptation of the adversary, and the choice of the individual. The avenue of inspiration from the Holy Spirit is to and through the spirit of man. The avenue of temptation from the adversary is to and through the physical body. The spirit is pure and would do right; the body is corrupt and subject to evil influence. These two forces are at war one with another. Which one dominates determines the character of the person, and his ultimate destination. If the spirit can completely dominate the body and the individual subjects his will to that of the Father, he may enter His presence and live with Him. If the spirit succumbs to the carnal influences of the body, the influence of the divine will is lost, and the person, in spite of fervent desire, has not the power to escape the domination of Satan.

For the flesh lusteth against the Spirit, and the Spirit against the flesh: and these are contrary the one to the other. (Galatians 5:17)

> *For the natural man is an enemy to God, and has been from the fall of Adam, and will be, forever and ever, unless he yields to the enticings of the Holy Spirit, and putteth off the natural man and becometh a saint through the atonement of Christ the Lord, and becometh as a child, submissive, meek, humble, patient, full of love, willing to submit to all things which the Lord seeth fit to inflict upon him, even as a child doth submit to his father.* (Mosiah 3:19)

The highest level to which man can attain in mortality is to so control his bodily appetites and passions, and so subject himself to the influence of the Almighty that his life becomes an expression of the will of the Father. The lowest level to which a man can fall in mortality is to so give in to the temptation to satisfy bodily appetites and passions and to thus gratify carnal desires as to become completely subject to the will of the Adversary.

> *And therefore, he that will harden his heart, the same receiveth the lesser portion of the word; and he that will not harden his heart, to him is given the greater portion of the word, until it is given unto him to know the mysteries of God until he know them in full.*
>
> *And they that will harden their hearts, to them is given the lesser portion of the word until they know nothing concerning his mysteries; and then they are taken captive by the devil, and led by his will down to destruction. Now this is what is meant by the chains of hell.* (Alma 12: 10-11)

"The chains of hell" is a euphemism frequently used in the scriptures to depict the power of the influence of the adversary over those who do not resist his influence. There comes a time for such individuals when there is no escape.

> *For behold, if ye have procrastinated the day of your repentance even until death, behold, ye have become subjected to the spirit of the devil, and he doth seal you his; therefore, the Spirit of the Lord hath withdrawn from you, and hath no place in you, and the devil hath all power over you; and this is <u>the final state of the wicked</u>.* (Alma 34:35)

One of the prime purposes of mortality is to provide an environment and a time and an opportunity for the spirit to overcome the flesh—for the individual to become the master of himself, to learn to control his actions, his words and his thoughts, and then to subject all these to the will of the Father.

> *For our <u>words</u> will condemn us, yea, all our <u>works</u> will condemn us; we shall not be found spotless; and our <u>thoughts</u> will also condemn us; and in this awful state we shall not dare to look up to our God; and we would fain be glad if we could command the rocks and the mountains to fall upon us to hide us from his presence.* (Alma 12:14)

So here are the three areas for the practice of mortality. The easiest of the three areas to control is our actions. But actions are the product of our thoughts, so we cannot control our actions without in some degree controlling our thoughts. Someone has said that "We sow in life a thought and for that thought we reap a word, and sowing a word, we reap an action, our actions make habits, our habits make our life and when this life is sown destiny or eternal life is our reward."

Avoiding an undesirable act takes different skills than overcoming a bad habit. There are many approaches to controlling our habitual actions, and much money is made promoting various approaches. All sorts of aids to appetite control are on the market. Each of these aids is in some way a substitute for willpower. Without the necessary willpower, when the aid is removed the undesired actions return. There is only one sure way to stop doing an undesirable thing, and that is to stop doing it. Decreasing by degrees is a decision not to stop. The consequences of an abrupt change of behavior may in some cases be difficult to endure, but there is just no way around it. Facing the consequences of change is part of the process of change.

Undesirable acts are usually the result of the temptation of the moment. Temptations of the moment always have some emotional involvement. After one's emotions are aroused it is very difficult to be objective in controlling behavior. Tempting circumstances must be envisioned and plans developed for the proper course of action <u>before</u> becoming involved in the situation.

James devotes an entire chapter in his general epistle to the powerful effect for evil that the things which we say may have. In Luke we read;

> *A good man out of the good treasure of his heart bringeth forth that which is good; and an evil man out of the evil treasure of his heart bringeth forth that which is evil: for of the abundance of the heart his mouth speaketh.* (Luke 6:45)

Some vain people dress in the most elegant clothing in order to impress those around them, then they sully their image with foul and unbecoming language, often unaware that they are seen more for how they speak than for how they dress.

How carefully we should guard our words that they may not injure another. Several years ago I had the privilege of viewing the painting, "Whistler's Mother," which was on loan from the Louvre in Paris, France, to the National Art Gallery in Washington, D.C. The painting, which is nearly life-size, was located in a prominent position near the entrance to the museum. It was surrounded by a red velvet cord about two inches in diameter, suspended from gold-colored posts; and standing near the painting was an armed guard! He was apparently protecting the painting from being damaged by some possibly deranged person with evil intent. It was hard to imagine that a guard was needed to protect the painting, which, in reality, was only a two-dimensional representation of some real person. Yet, how often do we do damage to the character and reputation of real people by thoughtless or malicious statements about them? We seem to have more concern for the representation than for the thing that it represents.

Some may believe that there is no harm in thinking unclean thoughts as long as they are not given expression. However, since out of *the abundance of the heart the mouth speaketh,* and since actions are the expressions of thoughts, how dangerous an exercise! But our thoughts are not all that private. He who is the Judge of all knows all the thoughts and intents of the heart. (Alma 18:32; D&C 6:16)

The most difficult area of self-domination is thought control. How many of us feel bad for harboring unclean thoughts, yet they linger and reappear to our continued consternation? In the first place, you cannot <u>try to forget</u> something, for in the trying you are remembering. Try this experiment with the class: Ask them not to think about an elephant for one minute. During that minute describe the elephant they are not supposed to think about—its long trunk and ivory tusks, its legs the diameter of telephone poles and its body like a huge barrel. Then ask what they have been thinking about; undoubtedly, the elephant. Next ask the class to think about a lion for one minute, and during this time describe the lion. Then ask the class if during that minute they were thinking about an elephant. You can explain that undesired thoughts are removed by replacing them with desirable thoughts.

It may be well to point out that living in the most wicked of all worlds, evil is all around us. We cannot avoid its confrontation from time to time. We should avoid evil environments to the extent possible, but they can never be completely avoided. We are counseled that we should be in the world but not of the world. Our senses are exposed to our environment from which we often receive unclean and unwanted information. However, the most important thing is how we process the information we receive. It may be well to point out that there is a difference between seeing and looking, between hearing and listening, between touching and feeling, between tasting and savoring. The first item of each pair is a reaction to our environment; the second item is an action on our environment.

As we gain control over our thoughts, words and actions we may arrive at the point where we *could not look upon sin save it were with abhorrence.* (Alma 13:12) Some may think that this is an unachievable goal, but the same scripture tells us that *there were many, exceedingly great many, who were able to achieve this sanctified condition.*

Even then, we may not relax our vigil. This life is a continual exercise in self domination. That is one of its main purposes. Our task should be, living one day at a time, to profit from our mistakes and gain strength by overcoming ourselves day by day. As we attempt to do so, we will have the Holy Spirit for our guide, and receive the strength that we need from a loving Father in Heaven.

—Gramps

CAN I DO TEMPLE WORK
WHILE DATING A NON-MEMBER?

Dear Gramps:

I'm 19, still unendowed and stuff but I do baptisms at the temple all the time. The trouble is that in the last few weeks I've started a relationship with a non-member. We're just really, really good friends, no bad stuff or immorality or anything, but I'm worried—can you still do temple work if you're dating a non-member? Thanks...

Sarah

Dear Sarah,

We are commanded to be in the world but not of the world. If we are involved in sacred activities such as temple work neither can we nor should we isolate ourselves from the rest of humanity. By the nature of our association with those outside the Church we may influence them, primarily by the power of a worthy example, to understand and accept the principles of the Gospel of Jesus Christ.

However, I would hasten to point out, that participating in temple work or not, there is a certain danger in having a "relationship" with a non-member. Friendships between two people of the opposite sex in their late teens cannot remain platonic for long. Having entered into such a relationship the emotional factors cannot be neglected, and they provide a powerful factor influencing our thinking and the judgments we make.

Let's say that you have espoused the noble goal of being married in the temple. You develop a close "friendship" with a very nice, honorable non-member young man. You have already determined that you will not marry him, so your relationship is defined as being purely temporary. However, as the bonds of affection grow, you begin to examine the possibility of converting him to the Church. That may not progress as fast as you would like, so the next step is to rationalize that after you get married you will have a greater influence, and then he would join the Church so that you could then go to the temple together. Then it becomes a tug of war of whose will is the strongest, whose commitment is the deepest, whose desire for family unity is the greatest, etc., etc.

It is true that in some split marriages the non-member joins the Church. It is also true that in many cases the faithful member adopts the lifestyle and the thinking of the non-member partner, and the member terminates her or his activity in the Church, with all the negative consequences for them and their posterity.

The question that perhaps you should ask yourself is, "How much am I willing to risk for my eternal exaltation to the highest degree of glory that may be achieved by our Father's children in the eternities?" That unspeakable goal is now within your grasp. You will marry soon, and you will marry someone with whom at one time you had a first date. How wise it would be to date only candidates for exaltation. You know who they are.

I would suggest that you maintain your friendship with the young man in question and with others, but the idea of starting a "relationship" immediately leads in the direction of an "exclusive relationship," a thing to be avoided at all costs.

—Gramps

ARE CHURCH LEADERS INFALLIBLE?

Gramps,
My question relates to, Aren't our leaders fallible sometimes? There are those who have some real problems understanding how it is that God can let us have imperfect leaders. I feel like I've answered that for myself before, since I know I would be lost without their help, but how do I answer this for others?
Rachel

Dear Rachel,

To the question, "Aren't our leaders fallible sometimes?" the answer is, "Of course they are." There has been and there will yet be only one infallible person to have ever lived on the earth. So I assume that the question really is, how could a bishop make a mistake or exercise poor judgment if he has the priesthood and the right to inspiration and revelation in conducting the affairs of his office?

There is no doubt in my mind that our bishops and other leaders receive both revelation and inspiration in conducting the affairs of their offices. But let's examine the question in some detail.

Let's assume that the bishop feels inspired to call a young man to be the Scout master. So he calls the man in for an interview and learns that he works the swing shift every day and could never attend any of the meetings. Could he have been inspired to select such a person? Of course he could. In the process of inspiration, we are *inspired* to use the information we have at hand in the best possible way. This young man was undoubtedly the most qualified and would benefit the most from the experience if only he would have been available. What the bishop needed in his case was a *revelation.* In other words, he needed to receive knowledge that he did not possess. So why wouldn't the Lord have revealed this truth to him? The answer is, why would the Lord go to all that trouble when all the bishop had to do was to ask the man? That's what interviews are for. So what could have been taken for poor judgment was simply a lack of information.

Now it's perfectly feasible that, in such a situation, had it been within the province of the Lord, he could have inspired the bishop to ask the young man to quit his job and seek for another so that he might have the opportunity to fill the calling. The Lord could have great things in store for a person with sufficient faith to make the sacrifices necessary to respond to the bishop's invitation.

Further, it isn't that the bishop is a puppet on a string being controlled in his every movement. The scriptures tell us that

> *it is not meet that I should command in all things; for he that is compelled in all things, the same is a slothful and not a wise servant; wherefore he receiveth no reward. Verily I say, men should be anxiously engaged in a good cause, and do many things of their own free will, and bring to pass much righteousness; For the power is in them, wherein they are agents unto themselves. And inasmuch as men do good they shall in nowise lose their reward. But he that doeth not anything until he is commanded, and receiveth a commandment with doubtful heart, and keepeth it with slothfulness, the same is damned.* (D&C 58:26-29)

So the Lord's servants use their minds and intellects to bring to pass much righteousness. Being fallible mortals they will not always make the wisest choices, but they will grow by their experience and gain proficiency in the offices of their callings. There are undoubtedly many circumstances in which the Lord would be perfectly satisfied if any one of a number of decisions were made; one avenue being as good as the other. Consider, for example, the following scriptures:

> But, verily, I will speak unto you concerning your journey unto the land from whence you came. *Let there be a craft made, or bought, as seemeth you good, it mattereth not unto me,* and take your journey speedily for the place which is called St. Louis. (D&C 60:5)
>
> And *it mattereth not unto me,* after a little, if it so be that they fill their mission, *whether they go by water or by land;* let this be as it is made known unto them according to their judgments hereafter. (D&C 61:22)
>
> And then *you may return to bear record, yea, even altogether, or two by two, as seemeth you good, it mattereth not unto me;* only be faithful, and declare glad tidings unto the inhabitants of the earth, or among the congregations of the wicked. (D&C 62:5)
>
> And let all the moneys which can be spared, *it mattereth not unto me whether it be little or much,* be sent up unto the land of Zion, unto them whom I have appointed to receive. (D&C 63:40)
>
> Wherefore, *go ye and preach my gospel, whether to the north or to the south, to the east or to the west, it mattereth not,* for ye cannot go amiss. (D&C 80:3)

So perhaps we shouldn't expect perfection, even if we were in a position to recognize it, from those who have the responsibility to exercise the callings of their offices. However, there is a serious obligation on the part of those over whom the bishop presides. When a person is sustained as a bishop by the congregation of the ward, that word *sustain* has a particular meaning. In the sustaining process we raise our arms to the square and make a covenant with the Lord that we will <u>sustain</u> (support, honor, accept, approve) the bishop in the office of his calling. That covenant is not a conditional covenant—"so long as he does what I think he ought to do," but our covenant is to sustain him in whatever decisions he makes. One wise General Authority said on one occasion, "Even a poor decision will work if the people will get behind it." Rather than us judging the bishop for the quality of his decisions, I imagine that the Lord will judge us for the quality of our obedience to priesthood authority.

The Lord recognizes and honors the sacred authority that he delegates to his servants. He will thus sustain the decisions that are made, and hold

the members accountable for their obedience. He has clearly and unequiv-
ocally stated that

> What I the Lord have spoken, I have spoken, and I excuse not myself;
> and though the heavens and the earth pass away, my word shall not pass
> away, but shall all be fulfilled, _whether by mine own voice or by the voice
> of my servants, it is the same._ (D&C 1:38)

I am of the opinion that we should obey our priesthood leaders in the
same manner that we would if the Lord himself were acting in that position.
It appears that those who have problems with imperfect leaders should
rather concentrate on trying to be perfect followers. If they do well, their
turn will come, and they will be grateful for the loyal support of those
whom they have the honor to serve.

—Gramps

DO THE ANXIOUS PRAYERS OF PARENTS ROB WAYWARD CHILDREN OF THEIR FREE AGENCY?

Dear Gramps,

_I have an inactive son who is 26. He is bothered by the fact that parents
seem to be able to pray for their children and then the children's lives
change (Alma). He feels that this deprives them of their free agency. If a
righteous parent prays for a wayward child, and then the child changes and
comes back to the church, has the child been deprived of his free agency?
Thanks,_

West Valley Mom

Dear West Valley Mom,

Free agency is one of the greatest gifts of God to man, and it is of such
a nature that it can never be compromised by man. What is free agency? An
agent is one who is authorized to act for or in the place of another. Thus, he
would have a certain authority to act, and a given responsibility to the person or organization for his actions. A 'free' agent is one who would have
no specific assignment, but would still be responsible for his actions. Thus,
the free agency given to us by the Father gives us the freedom to make
choices and the responsibility to God for the choices that we make.

To make choices we must be faced with alternatives. We are responsible to God only for the alternatives that are open to us. If, for instance, we
were held prisoner, we may wish to be free, but the choice would not be

open to us. On the other hand, we may have strong influences enticing us in one direction or another, and thus we would be required to make a choice. Whatever the choice, we would be responsible before God for the choice that was made.

If the Lord were to respond to the earnest prayer of a devoted parent in behalf of a wayward child, He may provide every opportunity and benign influence for the child to return to righteousness. But the child would yet be free to accept or reject any influences placed before him, and would be responsible for his choice. There is a hymn that includes these words:

> Know this, that every soul is free
> To choose his life and what he'll be.
> For this eternal truth is given,
> God will force no man to heaven.
> He'll call, persuade, direct aright,
> In numerous ways be good and kind,
> But never force the human mind.

Your son need never fear that he will ever be forced to be good, or to accept a given persuasion. Such a thing is contrary to the nature of man and to the will of God. Alma's son was duly impressed by the powerful influence of the angel that appeared before him, and as a result, chose to repent and be obedient. However, Laman and Lemuel, prayed over devoutly and fervently by their father, were visited by angels on numerous occasions and witnessed their mighty power, such that they were caused to quake in great alarm. However, they exercised their free agency in choosing to ignore the divine influence and continue in their own destructive paths.

We should continue to pray for our children, and if they respond to the Divine influence they will know that they had been free to do so.

—Gramps

WHAT DOES IT MEAN THAT THE AARONIC PRIESTHOOD HOLDS THE KEYS TO THE MINISTERING OF ANGELS?

Dear Gramps,
When John the Baptist restored the Aaronic Priesthood to Joseph Smith and Oliver Cowdery, one of the very few instructions he gave on that priesthood was that it "holds the keys of the ministering of angels..." As one who grew up in the Church and as an adult worked in the Aaronic Priesthood

quorums as instructor, I have noticed that there are very little, if any, instructions given to Aaronic Priesthood holders about using the key to the ministering of angels. Do you know why this is true? Or is it just me?
Kurious in Korea

Dear Kurious,
First we should consider, with whom do angels converse and to whom do they minister? It would be difficult to believe that angels approach those who are steeped in sin or who are troubled because of unworthiness. When a person is baptized he receives the Gift of the Holy Ghost. This gift is manifest only according to the righteousness of the individual. If, after baptism, he commits further sin, the Holy Spirit would withdraw and he would be left to himself until he had thoroughly repented and had been forgiven.

The Aaronic Priesthood has the authority to administer the ordinance of baptism, by which the repentant are forgiven of their sins. Being thus cleansed, they are in a position to receive the influence of the Holy Spirit and the ministering of angels. Further, the Aaronic Priesthood administers the emblems of the atonement by which the baptismal covenant is renewed, and through which the contrite and repentant are again forgiven of their sins. Thus, the Aaronic Priesthood holds the keys to the ministering of angels by holding the keys to those ordinances through which sin may be forgiven, and the person emerge worthy of the guidance and direction provided by the Lord through His ministering servants.

For a thorough discussion on this subject see the October 1998 Conference address of Elder Dallin H. Oaks, *Ensign*, Nov. 1998, pp. 37-39.
—Gramps

IS THE BAPTISM OF A MINOR CHILD WITHOUT PARENTAL CONSENT VALID?

Dear Gramps,
If a minor is baptized in the Church without parental consent is it legal with the church? Thank you.
Julia

Dear Julia,
The family is the fundamental unit of the Church. All other church organizations exist to support the family and the individual. Children are taught that they should be obedient to their parents. Paul counsels,

Children, obey your parents in all things: for this is well pleasing unto the Lord. (Colossians 3:20)

In addition, parents are the legal guardians of their children, and as such have rights and responsibilities for their welfare under the law. There may be two principal reasons why parents would object to having their children baptized in The Church of Jesus Christ of Latter-day Saints. One, they may firmly believe in another religion, and thus would feel that their child is doing something that is wrong, and that would not be to their benefit. The other principal reason is that they may be misinformed about the doctrine and practices of The Church of Jesus Christ of Latter-day Saints, and thus fear that their child may become involved in an organization that in some way would be detrimental to them.

Perhaps our best approach would be to recognize and show support for parental authority, to make friends with the parents and help them to develop an interest in learning more about the Church. Nothing could benefit any member of a family more than to have the entire family as a unit gain testimonies of the truthfulness of the gospel and to be baptized together.

If there does occur a circumstance where a minor child is baptized without those responsible being aware of the parent's objections, an appropriate accommodation would be made. My understanding is that if the parents were to require that the baptism be revoked, their demand would be honored, and the baptism would be considered as null and void.

—Gramps

THE PRINCIPLE OF SACRIFICE IN SUPPORTING THE WORK OF THE LORD

Gramps,
We are having financial problems—boy on mission, kids at school—and yes, we pay our tithing and offerings! We have managed but it has been just barely! What do you suggest for the future?
Arnold

Dear Arnold,
No doubt this is something that you need to talk to your bishop about. However, there are great blessings associated with the willingness to sacrifice. I have seen numbers of missionaries come into the field with nothing

more than the clothes on their backs. Their families couldn't even provide them with a suit. I know of one missionary who worked for five years selling popcorn to get enough money to begin his mission. Though we may feel that we can barely get by, we will get by, and the greater sacrifice brings the greater blessings. Make sure your bishop knows your circumstances and listen to and follow his advice and there is no doubt that you will be able to make your way.

—Gramps

WHAT WILL HAPPEN IN THE RESURRECTION TO PEOPLE WITH DONATED ORGANS?

Dear Gramps,

I was wondering what the church's position is on donating organs? I'm thinking in terms of the resurrection. Won't the body be made whole again even if an organ had been donated to save another life? Thanks in advance for your answer.

Debbie

Dear Debbie,

Are we questioning the power of the Creator to restore from the elements that which He created? The scriptures are generally silent on the process by which the Lord does His great work, very probably because it is far beyond the understanding of men. However, we do know that because of his infinite power even the very elements obey the voice of his command. In the various steps of creation mentioned in Abraham, Chapter 4, we read "And the Gods said"—Then the response, "and it was so, even as they ordered." Although we don't know the mechanism by which the elements came together, we do know that it occurred.

During the Savior's ministry, the voice of His command controlled the elements of the raging sea, healed the sick, the lame and the blind, and caused the dead to live again. Could He not just as easily restore in the resurrection every part of the body to its perfect frame? We really don't need to know the mechanism, but it is vital that we exercise sufficient faith to believe the revealed word and know that all that the Lord has declared will come to pass, even as He said.

—Gramps

A Problem With Family Relations And Adopting A New Religion

Dear Gramps,

I have a question for you. I am a new convert to the church and I have been intensely involved in missionary work. In fact I am preparing now to go on a mission. But to my question. A friend of mine that is very interested in being a member of the church belongs to a polygamist family. The family in a sense is LDS, and he has read the Book of Mormon. But he knows what his family is practicing is not right and he wants to be baptized. He spoke to a stake president about his concerns and this stake president told him that if he were baptized that he could never see his family again and only communicate with them once a year (like at Christmas). My friend now will not give up his family for the church. Even though he believes it and has a testimony of the Book of Mormon he loves his family too. Help, Gramps, can you shed some light?

Ben Joe

Dear Ben Joe,

Congratulations on your new membership in the Church! It's wonderful to catch the spirit of the work and have a burning desire to share the marvelous blessings of the gospel with others. I'm sure that you'll become a devoted and dedicated missionary.

With respect to your friend, there are a couple of things to consider. You mentioned that the polygamist family is in a sense LDS. Many good people believe and practice many of the doctrines of the Church of Jesus Christ of Latter-day Saints without having a true allegiance to the church, so it may be a little strong to say that in a sense they are LDS. Perhaps a better phrase would be that they practice some or many of the doctrines of The Church of Jesus Christ of Latter-day Saints. Some of those who practice polygamy claim membership in the church, but of course that is a false claim since the practice of polygamy is contrary to laws of the gospel. As I'm sure you know, any member practicing polygamy would normally be excommunicated.

Now with respect to your friend's interview with the stake president. We must be careful in making judgments on the report of a confidential interview. The stake president's counsel may have been based on much more than the reported circumstance. But whatever the circumstances were, if indeed your friend's membership were dependent on a separation from his family, although it's easy to see what a difficult decision it would be, there is no question as to what decision should be made. The Savior has said that

> He that loveth father or mother more than me is not worthy of me: and he that loveth son or daughter more than me is not worthy of me. (Matthew 10:37)

I would suggest that you might counsel your friend to take his problem to the Lord and seek guidance and strength from the author of that statement. In the meantime, if you continue to show your friendship and your support of whatever decisions he would make in the matter, you would be a true friend, and the example of your faithfulness would undoubtedly be a powerful influence in helping him make the right decision.
—Gramps

WHAT IS THE CHURCH'S POSITION ON R-RATED MOVIES?

Dear Gramps,

I was wondering if the church has ever made an official statement about R-rated movies? I've always thought that we are not supposed to watch them, but I've heard that not watching R-rated movies is just a guideline—like not drinking caffeinated soda—and not a commandment. Thanks in advance!! Love,

Thalia,

Dear Thalia,

Fortunately, man is endowed with the Spirit of Christ, which some people call a conscience. This Spirit gives all men the ability to know the difference between right and wrong. In the words of President Joseph F. Smith,

> There is a spirit in man; and the inspiration of the Almighty giveth them understanding. It is this inspiration from God, proceeding throughout all his creations, that enlighteneth the children of men; and it is nothing more nor less than the spirit of Christ that enlighteneth the mind, that quickeneth the understanding, and that prompteth the children of men to do that which is good and to eschew that which is evil; which quickens the conscience of man and gives him intelligence to judge between good and evil, light and darkness, right and wrong. (Joseph F. Smith, *Gospel Doctrine*, p.66)

Now, you know that watching R-rated movies is not the thing to do. You just said that you always thought we are not supposed to watch them. What more do you need than that personal revelation from God to give you guidance in such matters? The Lord has given the following counsel in D&C 58:26-28,

> For behold, it is not meet that I should command in all things; for he that is compelled in all things, the same is a slothful and not a wise servant; wherefore he receiveth no reward. Verily I say, men should be anxiously engaged in a good cause, and do many things of their own free will, and bring to pass much righteousness; For the power is in them, wherein they are agents unto themselves. And inasmuch as men do good they shall in nowise lose their reward.

So if there never had been a word from church authorities on the subject, there would still not be the slightest license to indulge in that which is unwholesome and degrading. Nevertheless, we have received direct and specific counsel from the brethren in this matter. From President Ezra Taft Benson,

> We counsel you, young men, not to pollute your minds with such degrading matter, for the mind through which this filth passes is never the same afterwards. Don't see R-rated movies or vulgar videos or participate in any entertainment that is immoral, suggestive, or pornographic. Don't listen to music that is degrading. (*Teachings of Ezra Taft Benson*, p. 222)

And from a summary of the October, 1993 General Conference, we have the words of Elder H. Burke Peterson,

> And again I would exhort you that ye would come unto Christ and lay hold upon every good gift, and touch not the evil gift, nor the unclean thing. (Moro. 10:30)
>
> Satan, the very devil and father of all lies, has slowly and slyly lowered the social norms of morality to a tragic and destructive level. In magazines and books, on CD's and tapes, on our television and theater screens is portrayed more and more often a lifestyle that might even rival the excesses of those who lived in Sodom and Gomorrah. The screens, music, printed materials, etc., are filled with a profusion of sex, nudity and vulgarity. Have the courage to turn it off in your living room. Throw the tapes and publications in the garbage can, for that is where we keep garbage. I know it is hard counsel we give when we say that movies that are R-rated and many with PG-13 ratings are produced by satanic influences. Our standards should not be dictated by the rating system. (*Church News, The Conference Issues*, October 9, 1993, p.16)

Now as to whether not watching R-rated movies is just a guideline or a commandment, does it really make any difference? I would think that any word from the Lord or from his appointed servants should be taken in a most serious manner. Brigham Young had this to say on that subject,

> Supporting the point that Section 89 was binding on the members of the Church, Brigham Young said on April 7, 1869, I know that some say the revelations upon these points are not given by way of commandment. Very well, but we are commanded to observe every word that proceeds from the mouth of God. (*Discourse of Brigham Young*, pp 182-83)

We live in a particularly dangerous age. Through the cunning of Satan, many things that are offensive in the sight of the Lord have become socially acceptable, and those whose high standards of conduct do not permit them to participate are branded a bigots or as prejudiced against 'civil' liberties. The day has fully come that was spoken of by Isaiah, in which he charged,

> *Woe unto them that call evil good, and good evil; that put darkness for light, and light for darkness; that put bitter for sweet, and sweet for bitter.* (Isaiah 5:20)

—Gramps

WHAT IS THE SIGNIFICANCE OF THE PHRASE, "THE RIGHT HAND OF GOD?"

Dear Gramps:

We had a lesson in Sunday School and we discussed being on the right hand of God. This was called the dexteral hand of God. Is there a significance and a spiritual meaning for this? Thanks for your help.

Tawnya

Dear Tawnya,

As most people are right-handed, the right hand is the favored of society, and the word for right-handedness has indicated this. In English, "right" means "correct." The right hand is the correct hand. The word "left" comes from the German "lucht," which comes from the left hand being weaker in most persons.

The English word "dexterity" comes from the Latin "dexteritat," which is defined as mental skill or quickness, especially skill and ease in using the hands. The word for the right hand in Spanish, which comes from the Latin, is "diestra," which means "wise" or "with ability." On the other hand (so to speak) the word for "left hand" in Spanish is "siniestra," which comes from the Latin "sinistr," which means "unlucky" or "inauspicious." "Sinistr" in English is "sinister," which is defined as presaging ill fortune or trouble, or accompanied by or leading to disaster.

People are generally suspicious of those who are different from them. Children often make cruel fun of others that are handicapped in some way. So the left-handed person, being different, has been designated as weak or sinister.

As a parenthetical note, it is interesting to contemplate how little consideration is given to those who are unfortunate enough to be left-handed. In this day and age, when minorities of all types are given great respect, the left-handed people remain alone without a support group or without consideration for their "handicap." As examples, men's shirts must be buttoned with the right hand. The only reason that women's blouses are buttoned from the left is that when buttons were invented only the richer could afford them, and the buttons were placed so the maids who dressed the ladies could do up the buttons with their right hands. Although possible, it's difficult to find such things as left-handed scissors. Mugs with inscriptions on them are all made so they may be read while holding the mug in the right hand. If you hold a pencil that has an inscription on it in your left hand, the inscription will be upside down. Left-handers must learn to adjust to and live in a right-handed world.

Now, whether the Lord is left-handed or right-handed is not known, but his parables, allegories and metaphors are related to and taken from the mores and norms of the people. In His parables He spoke of the mustard seed, the barren fig tree, the fisherman's net, the goodly pearl, the piece of money, the oil in the lamps, the wedding feast, the house on the rock, the leaven in the lump, and of the sheep and the goats. The sheep, which are of higher value and greater worth, he put on his right hand; and the goats, of lesser value and lesser worth, on his left. All this was done to teach lessons from objects and circumstances that were familiar to the people and in accordance with their beliefs, habits and practices.

So I believe that the right hand, the 'dextrous' hand, has no more intrinsic worth than does the left, and that the 'right hand of God' merely reflects the preconditioned notions of the people. To be on 'the right hand of God' immediately implies acceptance, not because the right hand has some spiritual connotation, but because it is immediately understood by the people, in particular the right handed majority, to be the favored place.

—Gramps

Should The Sacrament Be Taken Only With The Right Hand?

Dear Gramps,

While on splits with the missionaries this week our investigator asked us, "Is it true that you have to take the sacrament with only your right hand?" This is not the first time that I have heard of this. In fact once I took the sacrament tray in my right hand and took the bread with my left hand and someone told me that I took it wrong. Isn't taking the sacrament taking the sacrament? I don't think there is a special way to take it. I just thought I would ask you, Gramps!

BenJoe

Dear BenJoe,

The sacrament is one of the most sacred ordinances in which we can participate. The sacramental prayers were given by revelation, and are recorded in both the Book of Mormon and the Doctrine and Covenants. Since they are prayers revealed by the Lord, they must be given as they were received, word for word. As you are aware, the bread and water taken by the congregation are symbolic of the body and the blood of the Savior, and as they are taken they are reminders to us of the infinite suffering of the Lord as he assumed the responsibility to satisfy the demands of justice in payment for all of the sins that have been committed by all of mankind.

The effectiveness of that sacrifice in the payment for sin, however, is conditional on repentance by the individual and on the fulfillment of covenants made in the waters of baptism. It is appropriate during the taking of the sacrament to remember and renew the covenants we made when we were baptized. The baptismal covenant may be considered to have three parts: 1) we promise by covenant to take upon ourselves the name of Jesus Christ; 2) we promise to obey his commandments; and 3) we promise to remain true and faithful all the days of our life.

It is well to be reminded each week of that sacred obligation, so that we may keep it in the forefront of our minds to help us to be worthy of the guidance of His Holy Spirit to keep us unspotted from the sins of the world.

This sacred ordinance needs to be conducted with the utmost reverence, and those who administer the sacrament and who pass it to the congregation should do nothing that would detract from the sacred nature of the ordinance. It would be appropriate for them to be clean and to wear clean clothing, with hair well groomed and neatly combed. The priesthood members who officiate at the sacrament desk and who pass the sacrament to the congregation are encouraged to wear white shirts and ties, and to comport themselves in a reverent manner.

Now there is nothing in the scriptures that dictates the manner of dress or the specifics of deportment. So the way we dress is a matter of personal taste. Some young men may not possess a white shirt, and wearing one of color in those circumstances is perfectly acceptable. These norms have developed as acceptable customs appropriate to the sacredness of the ordinance. However, they are customs, not rules.

So it is with those who take the sacrament. It is customary to take the sacrament with the right hand; but this is a custom and not a rule. It is not the outward appearance but the mental process that gives meaning to the sacrament.

—Gramps

WHY SHOULD WE NOT WEAR MASKS ON HALLOWEEN?

Dear Gramps,

I would like to know where I can find out why LDS people don't wear masks on Halloween. I have heard all the time this is not what LDS people do and can't find any place that says why we don't cover our faces, and I'm not sure how to answer the question when it is asked of me by non-members. Can you tell me the answer to this question? Thank you.

Eva

Dear Eva,

I have not been able to find any material written by the brethren commenting on the wearing of Halloween masks. However, I am aware that it is the practice of the Church that masks are not to be worn at church-sponsored Halloween functions.

I would surmise that the reason for such a practice is directed toward the young people, some of whom might feel that they would have some license for inappropriate behavior if their identity were not known.

—Gramps

IS THE YEAR 2000 THE BEGINNING
OF THE MILLENNIUM?

Hey Gramps,

Thanks for your hard work and dedication to this page. You are making a difference. I don't know how many questions you get from us here in England but here goes. There is a lot of talk on Christ's Second Coming (no, really?) and how soon it is going to be here. Am I right in saying that when He comes there will be another 1000 years of His personal ministry on the earth before the final judgment, and that we are currently in the thousand years spoken of where Satan has free reign after which he will be bound?

Secondly, besides things like food storage, debt clearance, spiritual cleansing etc, as far as personal preparation is concerned, has the Church issued any special warnings for the end of 1999 and the beginning of the year 2000? Is the end of this year really going to be as tumultuous as they say? Look forward to hearing from you. Cheers.

Chris

Dear Chris,

Yes, the scriptures are clear that Christ will reign personally on the earth during the Millennium. If fact, the 10th Article of Faith says—

> We believe in the literal gathering of Israel and in the restoration of the Ten Tribes; that Zion (the New Jerusalem) will be built upon the American continent; that Christ will reign personally upon the earth; and, that the earth will be renewed and receive its paradisiacal glory.

And we read in Revelations that

> Blessed and holy is he that hath part in the first resurrection: on such the second death hath no power, but they shall be priests of God and of Christ, and shall reign with him a thousand years. (Revelation 20:6)

Concerning special instructions from the Church concerning the rollover into Y2K, I know of no specific instructions. The general authorities have been warning us for over 60 years to be prepared for difficult times. If we have followed the counsel of the brethren there will be no need to fear. However, if we wait until there is a pending disaster, we may be compared with the five foolish virgins, who brought no oil for their lamps.

I rather doubt that passage into the year 2000 will bring major catastrophic disruptions, but no doubt they are upon us and

> Not many days hence and the earth shall tremble and reel to and fro as a drunken man; and the sun shall hide his face, and shall refuse to give light; and the moon shall be bathed in blood; and the stars shall become

exceedingly angry, and shall cast themselves down as a fig that falleth from off a fig-tree. And after your testimony cometh wrath and indignation upon the people. For after your testimony cometh the testimony of earth-quakes, that shall cause groanings in the midst of her, and men shall fall upon the ground and shall not be able to stand. And also cometh the testimony of the voice of thunderings, and the voice of lightnings, and the voice of tempests, and the voice of the waves of the sea heaving themselves beyond their bounds. And all things shall be in commotion; and surely, men's hearts shall fail them; for fear shall come upon all people. (D&C 88:87-91)

—Gramps

SHOULD I GIVE UP MY CHURCH ACTIVITY TO KEEP PEACE IN MY MARRIAGE TO MY INACTIVE HUSBAND?

Dear Gramps,

When I married my husband—a returned missionary, he was a very faithful member of the church. But, now, he is quite bitter and very resentful of any time or means that I contribute to the church. This is causing an enormous amount of friction in our marriage. I love the church. I am happiest when serving others and making financial contributions. My husband is a very good person. He is kind, thoughtful, helpful, but he resents the church. Should I be sneaky, deceitful? Should I give up doing church service, taking food to neighbors? Please help me with my marriage yet my commitments to God?

vg, from Idaho

Dear vg,

I can imagine how difficult it would be for you to be obedient to the gospel when that obedience would be resented by your husband. But we live in an imperfect world, where apparent inequities abound. Such difficulties, however, help us to establish the proper priorities in our lives. Although your husband is bitter about the church, yet our Heavenly Father loves him and is as interested in his welfare as in that of anyone else. Reflect for a minute on the one lost sheep and the other ninety and nine.

Now, if you were to follow your husband's desires and leave the Church with him, do you think that either of you would ever come back? Not likely. However, if you maintain your fidelity to the Lord and to the gospel, being neither sneaky nor deceitful, and yet are kind and loving to your husband, your example will be a powerful influence in his life to help him overcome his difficulty. The Lord told us that our allegiance to him has priority over our allegiance to anyone else.

He that loveth father or mother more than me is not worthy of me: and he that loveth son or daughter more than me is not worthy of me. And he that taketh not his cross, and followeth after me, is not worthy of me. (Matthew 10:37-38)

If he is the wage earner and chooses not to pay tithing, that is his prerogative. If you have separate incomes, you should reserve the right to pay tithing on that which you earn. Also, to try to convince your husband to change his ways is generally a fruitless effort, and would result in additional discord in the family. It is incumbent upon you to respect your husband and his way of life. You could then, with added justification, follow your own way of life. If you maintain fidelity to your own covenants and commitments to the Lord, and do so without hesitation, without deviation and without fanfare, always appealing to your Father in Heaven to soften your husband's heart toward those things that he once held dear, you will exert a powerful influence for good that sooner or later will bring him to his senses, so that he may again enjoy the peace and blessings of the Holy Spirit.

—Gramps